PGG
Personal Growth Gab

Thought-provoking, inspirational
and entertaining essays to keep you
connected with yourself and make
sense of this journey called Life.

VOLUME ONE

KRISTINA

D1247561

Personal Growth Gab (PGG), Volume One: Thought-provoking, inspirational and entertaining essays to keep you connected with yourself and make sense of this journey called Life.

Authored by Kristina Leonardi, edited by Elise Goldberg, designed by Christina Quintero

Logos designed by Michalis Galanis and James Ricciardella

ISBN-13: 978-0692336960 (Custom Universal)

ISBN-10: 0692336966

For my clients, seminar attendees
and weekly email readers:

You continue to enrich my life by
providing numerous opportunities for
me to express myself, and the honor
of using the best parts of me to work
with the innermost parts of you.

THANK YOU

Because the acorn does not

become an oak tree overnight

A journey of a thousand miles

begins with a single step

The caterpillar must turn

to goop before it can become

a butterfly

And everything happens

in time and on time

To create peace in your piece

of the pie

—Kristina Leonardi

TABLE OF CONTENTS

Foreword ix

Introduction xi

How to Use This Book xiv

PGGs Divided by Theme xvi

Self-Expression 1

The Journey 45

Self-Love & Care 79

Challenging Times 105

Self-Reflection 133

Change & Transition 167

Current Events & Global Perspective 187

Love 229

Head vs. Heart 245

Communication & Connection 259

Women's Empowerment 285

Presence, Process & Patience 299

Mixtape Collection 325

PGG Playlists 328

PGG at the Movies 334

Aha Moments / To-Do List / Notes 336

Index 340

Acknowledgments 343

About the Author 346

FOREWORD

Kristina gets it. She knows what's going on and isn't afraid to tie everything in: good old-fashioned common sense; timeless values like patience and love; philosophy, current events, and pop culture.

She reaches up toward the stars and explains how the forces of the Universe affect us in deep, profound ways and then brings us right back down to Earth using practical examples, humor and a healthy dose of music and movie references to show us how our lives really are connected and united by everything we know, things we don't, and things we take for granted. We have the power within us, and sometimes we just need someone to point it out.

What Kristina does is help lead us to our perfect guides: ourselves.

—Monica Chelchowski Hens,
PGG reader and fan from Day One

INTRODUCTION

When I started Personal Growth Gab (the essays I refer to as PGGs) in January 2010, I wasn't really sure what I was doing or how it would develop. Nearly five years and 131 original essays/posts later I continue to find my voice, observe common themes, and muse upon life's lessons, sharing what I know to be true in a unique and entertaining way. This is my art and one of my gifts to the world— who knew?

I am *not* one of those quick, effortless writers or fancy word-smiths. I am moderately dyslexic. I barely read books. But I do have something to say, and these 500- to 900-word essays take me, on average, eight-plus hours to write and edit (as best I can!). They are a creative labor of love.

Between my clients, friends, family and own personal journey, along with paying attention to the planets and current events, I have been able to gain a special bird's-eye view and insight into many lives, and I assure you that you are not alone in having gone through a *lot* of inner and outer "stuff" along this journey called Life. Through these weekly PGGs, I connect the dots and try to articulate and illuminate what we're all experiencing to make your days a little better and brighter.

I am grateful to have this vehicle to express my thoughts, am honored that they are read by so many of you each week, and want to especially thank those who have taken the time to give me your feedback. It lets me know that the time and energy, and sometimes sweat and tears, I put into the PGGs each week are not in vain or wasted away in some digital black hole. And your overwhelmingly positive response ultimately inspired me to publish them in handy book form, along with some fun tidbits at the end, for you to access at any time.

Please note that since these started out as (and continue to be) a component of my business e-newsletter, they always end with a request for the reader to consider using the services of yours truly. I thought that would be some-what irritating to read repeatedly; however, besides being a subtle sales pitch, it is often the tidy, clever ending that ties the whole piece together and thus couldn't be left out. So instead, with the assistance of my intrepid editor Elise Goldberg, those final paragraphs have been altered to reflect a more personal ending and call to action with ways you can help yourself.

I hope you enjoy reading this book from cover to cover, by chapter when you are dealing with that specific topic, and/or by just opening to whatever page reveals itself to you—trusting that it is exactly what you need to read at that particular moment.

If you don't have a journal handy, there is room for notes and aha moments in the back, and since I reference (either overtly or subtly) lots of music and movies, I've put together a playlist of all that were mentioned or in my head at the time, so here you go ... I sincerely hope you enjoy, and even more important, benefit from, *PGG* in all its many forms!

Kristina

P.S. Want to be one of those lucky weekly email readers? Go to the contact page on KristinaLeonardi.com to join my mailing list. And don't forget to like "Personal Growth Gab" on Facebook, and follow me on Twitter @clearlykristina.

HOW TO USE THIS BOOK

There are lots of ways this book can be handy and help with whatever you are going through at any particular moment in your life.

The basics:

The book is divided by theme, so if you want to focus on, let's say, self-love, or you're dealing with change and transition ... boom! There's a whole category you can just read from beginning to end.

As any good DJ (or pre-iTunes baby) knows, songs can be grouped in a variety of ways to evoke a certain mood or communicate a specific message. Since most of the PGGs touch upon several themes, I've compiled some PGG "mixtapes" that might apply to a particular situation you're going through or question you might have. Check them out in the section called **Mixtape Collection.**

Or in that old-fashioned magical way, you can simply hold the book in your hands, close your eyes and ask yourself, "What is the most important thing for me to read right now?" and see what page you open to—it's never an accident!

Other stuff:

You'll notice that a lot of the PGGs reference music and/or movies, either through titles, lyrics or quotes, so I thought you'd enjoy separate playlists and a movie list.

See the **PGG Playlists** and **PGG at the Movies** sections after the **Mixtape Collection**. (That's also why you'll see those funky little numbers superscripted throughout the PGGs; they correspond to the **PGG Playlists**.)

Write it down:

Have an aha moment or want to make a note to yourself or quote something from a PGG? No problem—a few extra pages are included for you to do so. Writing is the best way to make something stick in your soul, so go for it!

Remember you are constantly changing and evolving, so some PGGs may be more relevant for you now than others. The great thing is that even though they have dates on them, they discuss timeless themes, so you never know what might hit you at any given moment or when you might "get" something the second or third time around.

In finishing this book, my amazing editor Elise brought this Christopher Morley quote to my attention. He wrote in his novel *Parnassus on Wheels*, "When you sell a man a book you don't sell him just 12 ounces of paper and ink and glue— you sell him a whole new life."

I am hoping you can glean a little insight into yours as a result of me sharing quite a bit of mine.

PGGs
DIVIDED BY THEMES

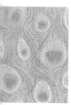

SELF-EXPRESSION 1

Service & Self
Lucky Charms
Of Pride & Prejudice
Your Epidermis Is Showing
USA
Don't Tread on Me
Write or Die
Labor Pains
At Your Service
Minute to Win It
Freedom Is Fashionable
V
And S/He Was
Work It
New Rules
Sing Out Loud
The Experiment
Shake Your Groove Thing
Own It
Election

THE JOURNEY 45

Groundhog Day, the Grammys & Gaga
Money Makes the World Go Round
Lost?
Steppin' Out
Leap of Faith
Going the Distance
The Price Is Right?
An Apple for the Teacher
What's Your Number?
Life Is Like a Box of Chocolates
Whoa, Nelly
Vision Quest
Life Class

SELF-LOVE & CARE 79

Discipline Is Not a Dirty Word
Tiptoe Through the Tulips
Smile in Your Liver
The Pleasure Principle
High Anxiety
Lighten Up
Chillax
One Is the Magic Number
Roots
A Body at Rest
Mommie Dearest

CHALLENGING TIMES 105

Sending Out an SOS
Thank the Turkeys Too!
You Are Not Alone
Out of Control
The Heat Is On/Under Pressure
The Roof Is On Fire
Fear Factor
Joni Mitchell Never Lies
Beauty in the Breakdown
You, Me & Dupree
Attitude of Gratitude

SELF-REFLECTION 133

The Passion of Passover
Slow Down, You Move Too Fast
Preparing for Liftoff
Summatime
Into the Woods
Holiday Road
Wherever You Go, There You Are
Blast from the Past
Freeze-Frame
Conjunction Junction
The Blind Side
Be Kind Rewind
Heart & Soul
Validation Nation
Drop It Like It's Hot
Happy

CHANGE & TRANSITION

CHANGE & TRANSITION...............167

Out With the Old, In With the New
The Year of Living Uncomfortably
Changing of the Guard
Something's Gotta Give
Don't Worry, Be Happy
The Change-Up
Let the Sun Shine In
Reality Bites

CURRENT EVENTS & GLOBAL PERSPECTIVE

CURRENT EVENTS & GLOBAL PERSPECTIVE.................187

Mercy Mercy Me
Déjà Vu All Over Again
For Weddings and a Funeral
Battle of the Bulge
Follow the Leader
A Tale of Two Streets
American Horror Story
Peas on Earth
World Wide Web
Get Up, Stand Up
All Roads: Same Place
You Say You Want a Revolution
They Might Be Giants
Beauty & the Beast
Grown-Ups

LOVE 229

Let Love Rule
Free Love
Just Desserts
All That You Can't Leave Behind
Love Saves the Day

HEAD VS. HEART 245

Girl Power
Polar Shift
Under the Sea
Just Go With It
(Wo)Man Up
A Fool's Errand
Truth No. 2

COMMUNICATION & CONNECTION 259

Apples & Oranges
To Tell the Truth
Like a Fish Needs a Bicycle
You've Got Mail
Jungle Love
Moonies, Mormons & Muslims
Six Seconds
Attachment Theory
People Who Need People
The Magic Touch

WOMEN'S EMPOWERMENT

WOMEN'S EMPOWERMENT 285

I Am Woman, Hear Me Roar
You've Come a Long Way, Baby?
Are You Gonna Go My Way?
Rage Against the Machine

PRESENCE, PROCESS & PATIENCE

PRESENCE, PROCESS & PATIENCE 299

New Year's Message: Don't Believe the Hype
Souper Douper
Snow Daze
One Day at a Time
The Present of Presence
Tangible Schmangible
Here Today, Gone Tomorrow
A More Perfect Union
The Patience of Patients
The Rhythm of the Saints
It Takes Two to Tango

SELF-EXPRESSION

Service & Self

January 19, 2010

Yesterday we celebrated the life of Martin Luther King Jr.— a day when we are asked to use our time and energy to serve others for the greater good. Wouldn't it be nice to know that the work you do every day has that effect?

If you're doing what you love, then chances are it is! When we express who we are and do what we love, others will automatically benefit—whether it's from the work itself or the positive vibes around us because we are happier and more fulfilled. Joy is contagious!

If you don't feel that way, then you are like many people who feel they need any job for a job's sake. But that is when we are least in harmony with who we are, and it causes much unnecessary stress and aggravation ... who needs that?!

Contrary to conventional wisdom, service can actually come from serving ourselves as much as we serve others.

If you are feeling frustrated or lost with your career and/ or transition and know you need a change, think of it as an opportunity to give a little boost, balance and direction to your career and life path. Because once you do, you can start sharing your unique gifts and talents with the world— we need you!

Lucky Charms

March 16, 2010

A rabbit's foot, a four-leaf clover, or that certain pair of underwear. We all have things in our life that we consider good luck charms—those objects we hold near and dear to bring us a little special magic in whatever situation we need it.

But what about your inner charms, the things that make you *you*, those little quirks, sayings and even physical characteristics that come together in a combination that's uniquely yours? This is where your true luck lies, and by using your charms and trusting where they take you, doors that were previously closed can start to miraculously open.

We spend more time and energy than we realize trying to fit in and conform to certain standards of acceptance. Whether it be in our work, family, relationships, appearance or lifestyle, most of us bury to varying degrees the very substance that will make us the most appreciated and successful. So if things aren't going your way right now, why not "let your freak flag fly" and see what happens?

Exploring the little treasures you possess and how to use them in the world can help you uncover those special gems that will lead to your pot of gold at the end of the rainbow!

Of Pride & Prejudice

April 6, 2010

In the movie *Clash of the Titans*, Perseus is half-man and half-god, a truly unique being bridging the worlds of Argos (humans) and Mount Olympus (the gods). He finds out about the Olympian part of him as an adult, when men are at war with the gods who were responsible for killing Perseus's beloved family.

Perseus is then enlisted in this battle, as he is deemed the only one who could give humans a victory precisely because of his special background. But Perseus refuses to utilize his god-power and the gifts that his father, Zeus, gave him because he despises the gods who ruled the land so mercilessly, and he would never consider himself one of them.

For much of the story, our hero is too proud to use all that he has been given and completely denies half of who he is—until he finally realizes that what he has is indeed exactly what mankind needed to defeat Hades. It was essential that Perseus get to the point of self-acceptance and just be, and by doing so, he prevented the destruction of humanity!

Now you may not be a revenge-seeking character in a remake of the sweeping tale of a kitschy '80s sort-of Greek mythology movie, but you do have a few things within you that are the keys to making you who you are and what you are meant to do! Once you discover and accept that, then the sky is the limit for you to soar. And by doing so, we will all benefit.

Your Epidermis Is Showing

June 8, 2010

When I was a kid, we used go around teasing each other as if this was some embarrassing declaration. Of course, the joke was that it's almost always showing, especially in the summer!

Our physical body is our face to the world, but it's not all of us. If we consider that our skin is the clothing for who we really are, then what do you look like naked? Does your inner self reflect what's on the outside, and vice versa?

Well, if you are a cast member of *Jersey Shore*, I would say the answer might be yes ... but when is exposing too much epidermis making up for a lack of something underneath? And what about what you wear on your body? This is also an extension and expression of your true self and has nothing to do with looking as if you stepped out of the latest issue of *Vogue*.

The goal is to be so in harmony with your thoughts, words and deeds that it shows in your personality, clothes and interactions with others. So save the masks and uniforms for Halloween or a TV reality show. The irony is that most of the time, transparency happens whether you like it or not—what's happening on the inside will automatically be seen on the outside.

So if you're not quite feeling that your magnificence is reflected in your Manolos, or that your substance is revealed in your Snooki bump or spray tan, maybe you need to take a look at yourself in a mirror (literally and figuratively), then allow your inner stylist to help every part of you shine!

USA

June 29, 2010

I had not paid much attention to the World Cup until last week, when I happened to catch the second half of the US-Algeria game. The best part was that I was watching it on Univision, so when the United States won, the emotional factor went off the charts with the Latin announcers scream-singing "GOOOOAAAALLLL," accompanied by the unbridled enthusiasm that only they can express about the *how and why* of the win, especially after the bad calls against them in previous games. La esperanza! La fe! El corazón sobre la forma! La lucha y el espíritu de este equipo que triunfo, que es justo!

If you don't speak Spanish, the gist is this: It was all about the spirit, determination, fight and heart of the team, not necessarily anything technical that got them the win. After that experience, I watched with excitement their dramatic game with Ghana three days later. Although they did not advance further, Team USA surely did not lose.

The flamboyant, gender-bending US Olympic figure skater Johnny Weir has had ups and downs throughout his career and his share of unfair marks from international judges. But he refused to be anything other than who he is, and he always excelled when he put the "Johnny" back into his performances, along with his love for the sport—and his costumes.

Although he did not bring home a medal from Vancouver, he skated his personal best and received incredible press, speaking engagements, his own reality TV show, and a bright future ahead. Because he worked extremely hard, remained genuine, and let his spirit shine through, Johnny surely did not lose.

What the soccer team and Weir have in common through their international competitions is that they represented the United States with passion and perseverance. In true American style, they embraced who they are, carried on in spite of all obstacles, and were victorious in their own ways.

In honor of our upcoming Independence Day, let your *Unique Spirit* and *Authenticity* overtake whatever you endeavor and see what happens. Find the moxie in your mojo and do whatever it takes to make your country proud!

Don't Tread on Me

July 6, 2010

Our founding fathers, mothers, cousins and friends infused our nation with extraordinary concepts of human evolution and the ideals of true freedom, and we have much to thank them for.

Their "greatest social experiment in history" has had its ups and downs, and our culture is in constant motion—good, bad or otherwise—because of it. Although we no longer exist beneath the thumb of our former rulers across the pond, we all live to some extent under the control of something or someone.

July, then, is a great time to step back from, reflect upon, and extricate yourself from whatever that might be—whether technology, bright shiny things, outdated relationships or ways of thinking, food or other substances, and the illusion of connectedness and fulfillment that they all give. Find your voice among all the white noise and distractions, replacing them with the enlightened, revolutionary spirit this country was founded on: your definition and assertion of Life, Liberty and the Pursuit of Happiness.

These times they are a changin', so in the Spirit of '76, take this month to also perform your own experiment and declare independence from blind obedience to conventional wisdom that may no longer be conventional or wise.

Don't let the rockets' red glare prevent you from seeing that you do indeed live in the land of the free, and that you can make your life a home of the brave.

Write or Die

August 31, 2010

I recently attended a workshop with Erica Jong, who implored us to write the story we absolutely had to tell or we would die. She also taught us to write something that unlocks who we are, encouraged us to be ourselves, and told us to discover and write in our own voice. But how do you know what your voice is if you never use it? (Sorry, but tweets and texts barely count, if at all!)

You don't need to be an aspiring blogger, poet or novelist to heed these wise words. I always recommend that folks write as much as they can to get in touch with their inner selves; a journal is a place where you can be truly free to express who you are and what you need to say. When you've connected honestly and often enough to that internal, emotional voice, you will begin to reveal who you are and what is important to you—whether in career, relationships or life in general. We write what we need to read.

A journal is a place to clarify your feelings, share your ideas and experiences, release the past, and make plans for the future, all without judgment. Your journal is your best friend. At the very least, it is a to-do list for items big and small. The act of writing something down makes it real and tangible, and it helps crystallize the hurricane of thoughts and emotions we often have swirling around inside us.

The process of putting it all on the page can make us more effective in communicating what we need or want from others or ourselves—and actually make sense doing so! I also suggest using a pen and paper whenever possible. It's more organic and raw when you take out the technological middleman.

If you access your authentic voice in writing, then, as Erica said, "being an author makes you an authority." You don't have to be the next Maya Angelou, J.D. Salinger or Danielle Steele to be the author of your own life and truth. So give writer's block the finger and just start putting pen to paper. You'll soon be on your way to your own personal best-seller list before you can say Pulitzer Prize!

Labor Pains

September 7, 2010

Earlier this summer after having dinner at a friend's house, I looked at her husband and told him he was pregnant. Not in the transgender, real-life man-mother way or the fictitious Arnold Schwarzenegger way, or even that joking ate-too-much way, but in that "there is something in you that is just waiting to be born," itching-to-see-the-light-of-day way. In fact, in some Latin languages "to give birth" is literally translated as "to give light."

Besides being a bookend for the season, Labor Day is the beginning of harvest time, of reaping what you have sown earlier in the year. Whatever it is you are trying to manifest, you need to be sure it is a labor of love, then dedicate yourself to the work necessary for it to come to fruition. And if you haven't already started, don't be sitting around waiting for an immaculate conception.

These things happen only with commitment, focus, time, energy and a bit of elbow grease. After the appropriate gestation period, persistence and deep breaths take you into the homestretch. No pain, no gain, as they say, and everywhere in Nature we see that the moment of birth requires an extra push to get through to the other side.

As for my friend, he needed to start doing more creative writing, which perhaps might yield a novel. At the very least, it would activate a part of him that was simply not being used in his day job or his role as husband and dad.

A favorite quote of mine comes from *The Prophet* by Khalil Gibran: "[T]o love life through labor is to be intimate with life's most inmost secret. ... *Work is love made visible.*"

What kind of "work" are you trying to give birth to? A special project, healthy lifestyle, your own business, solid relationships, bustling career, creative endeavors, expanding your family, or simply a new and improved version of you?

No matter what you desire to bring into being (yes, even an actual baby), you need to take on the role of metaphorical midwife, so you can welcome your bundle of joy into the world as easily and effortlessly as possible.

At Your Service

January 18, 2011

Life's most persistent and urgent question is: What are you doing for others? —Martin Luther King Jr.

One of the most common desires I hear from clients who are embarking on a new career or making a transition is that they want to do something with meaning, something that helps people.

My approach is to ask them: "What is the thing that makes you *you*? What you are passionate about; when do you lose track of time?" I inquire as to what their fantasy job would be, and very rarely does that answer have to do with becoming a social worker or joining the Peace Corps.

You don't have to be the next Mother Teresa, Gandhi or MLK to make a difference and live your life in service to others. Perhaps that is your path, but as Dr. King also said, "Everybody can be great because everybody can serve." Running for public office or volunteering on a regular basis can certainly fill that role, but service can be expressed in myriad forms that aren't always so obvious or grandiose. Just being yourself and doing your best at being YOU allows us to benefit from whatever unique gifts and talents you possess.

When one's work is done with love and integrity, every job is one of service. MLK Day is also about celebrating diversity, which can refer to many things, including one's occupation. Every job helps make the world go round. Whether it's the super taking care of your building, the bus driver making sure you get to your destination safely, the guy who makes your coffee and bagel every morning, the janitor who cleans the public restrooms you use, the designer of the clothes you are wearing, the comedian who made you laugh last night, the singer whose song you enjoyed on your iPod, or the writer whose novel you devoured over the weekend—no occupation is too insignificant. As long as their work was done to the best of their ability, it's easy to see how any of those people have served you on some level.

And regardless of your job, there is also the service you can provide by smiling at someone when you're walking down the street, or showing kindness to a stranger; you'll notice how, for a moment, you made someone happy or uplifted that person in some way.

The thing *I* enjoy most and lose track of time doing is talking to folks about their life's work and helping them make their everyday existence as meaningful and peaceful as possible. Helping people connect the dots of their life, create more work/life balance, and recognize the value in whatever they do is why I am here, at your service.

Minute to Win It

February 8, 2011

When I was in sixth grade, my elementary school presented the Norma Gold Human Relations Award to three students from our class of about 100. To my shock my name was called, and to this day it's one of my proudest achievements—mostly because I had absolutely no idea the award existed or that I had done anything special that warranted attention. I was just very involved and gave my all to whatever I did; at that young age, I unconsciously expressed the best version of who I was and got recognized for it.

I am not a competitive person and although athletic, I never wanted to play school sports for that very reason. But sometimes we need to have that extra bit of eyes-on-the-prize attitude to take us to the next level. In the movie *Remember the Titans*, a racially integrated football team comes together to be the undefeated champ of its division, a victory that was symbolic of so much more in the newly desegregated South. Prior to the final game, Denzel Washington, playing Coach Boone, declares: "I'm a winner. I'm going to win."

Every field has its pinnacle of achievement and earned recognition, so why not set your sights on one? In the midst of this season with the Grammys and Academy Awards on their way, it's a good time to consider: What is the equivalent of a Super Bowl, World Cup, Olympic medal, Emmy or Tony in your life? What's your version of the Nobel or

Pulitzer Prize? What would your criteria be and what would you call it?

Define in every area of life what your standard of excellence is that makes you a champion. Set that goal for yourself this year or for your bucket list—even if you never attain it, raising the bar for yourself can only make you better in every way.

The next step is to believe that you are worthy of the accomplishment. When Tango Diva held a contest for its 2007 Diva Visionary Award, *at the last minute* I decided to nominate myself. I then found out *after* the fact that—gulp— I would have to ask people to vote for me in addition to being judged. The whole process made me incredibly uncomfortable, but I realized that at some point I had to decide that I wanted to win—and that decision *took but a minute*. I figured I deserved it as much as anyone else and just had to go for it. And lo and behold, I WON!

Sometimes you have to seek the recognition (remember: producers run Oscar *campaigns*), make the commitment to it and push until you win, and sometimes it's a surprise that just falls in your lap. Regardless of how the victory comes, it won't occur without the intention of doing and being your best. And as you prove yourself and are honored along the way, know that once you win it, you must own it.

Don't think you have any horn to toot or mirror-ball trophy to win? Everyone excels in some area; the key is to promote your hidden superstar and find an arena for your unique MVP to shine!

Freedom Is Fashionable

February 15, 2011

It always seems a little off to me that Valentine's Day takes place during the astrological sign of liberty-loving, independent, eccentric Aquarius, characteristics more suited to a people's revolution or Grammy red carpet. With all that kind of energy in the air lately, freedom looks as good on Egyptians as it does on Lady Gaga.

Ever since the majority of humanity decided not to walk around in our birthday suits, we can, if we're lucky, have varying degrees of expression in how we cover our naked bodies. Right now we're in the midst of New York Fashion Week, which to many people it is a seemingly frivolous and fun affair. But the reality is that as long as there are options in what is acceptable for us to wear, there exists freedom in other areas—think of Mao suits, corsets, burqas and beards.

It's been 20 years since George Michael's classic video,[1] a time when we knew the models' names, they had meat on their bones, and the artist was nowhere in sight, wanting to liberate himself from the bubblegum image of his Wham! days. Today designers are more the rock stars, and perhaps appropriately so.

Devil Wears Prada masterminding and *Fashion Police* citations aside, the fashion industry produces its own version of freedom fighters, providing us with the garments we need to protect and express who we are. That, in turn, fuels an environment to pursue work we are passionate about, breeds a culture that is inclusive, gives us permission to love whomever we want, and most of all, enables us to enjoy the freedom to be ourselves.

Pop stars and celebrities can take this to the extreme; it requires more courageous souls to carry off a CeeLo or Nicki Minaj ensemble, but the more they push the boundaries of self-expression, the more they give us all permission to do the same.

Not sure if your style is more Bieber or Beyonce, rock 'n' roll or Rihanna? Uncover and unleash the inner you, and reflect it in your outer style, making the most of who you are, inside and out.

V

I will continue to use my voice, the one I was told is important and matters. —Rosario Dawson

I'm not a huge fan of *American Idol* but have watched it here and there, and the theme I noticed this season has to do with contestants "finding their voice" and being artists who are true to themselves. Now there's a new kid on the block called *The Voice*, and the *X Factor* is coming around the corner as well.

Although on one hand we are attracted to the idea of being plucked from obscurity and thrust into the spotlight, I think our more subconscious obsession with these shows stems from how powerful that little box in our throat really is, because not enough of us use it to its fullest potential.

I have a client who feels she is not heard by her boyfriend, another who is trying to find his voice in his job, another who gets stuck when trying to articulate anything about herself. Shania Twain, who has made a fortune living by her voice, lost it after the devastating news of her husband's betrayal and coming to terms with a traumatic childhood. Nothing is more effective in showing us just how essential our voice is to who we are than when it is not there.

I recently had the privilege of meeting one of the most distinctive and profound voices in our society today,

Dr. Cornel West, who was being honored, along with Rosario Dawson and former mayor David Dinkins, at the very aptly named Voices, the annual gala for The Brotherhood/Sister Sol, an organization that empowers low-income black and Latino youths to become agents of social change through education, activism and spoken word.

West, a frequent guest on mainstream TV talk shows, always has an intelligent and entertaining discourse with his host and speaks my kinda language about love, courage and shared humanity; he is an extremely unique voice of reason in a sea of media madness.

At the end of the event, the students' poem said you "can't sing when your guard is up and your mouth is closed. ... The consequences of silence are intolerable." No matter who you are, without your voice, and your Voice, you are lost.

The logo and ads for *The Voice* show two fingers in a V; I realized it's no small coincidence that this is also the sign of peace and victory, as they are all intertwined. Because when you find your Voice and use it, you feel at peace with yourself and can be Victorious in overcoming any obstacle— and that is Vital.

Whether you want to sing like Shania, speak out like Rosario and Cornel, or are from Madonna's generation or Gaga's, it's up to you to use what you have and see that you were Born This Way[2] so you can Express Yourself,[3] hey, hey ...

And S/he Was

May 17, 2011

Just when the caterpillar thought the world was over,
it became a butterfly. —Unknown

One of my current clients has done a tremendous amount of work in a very short time: She had major revelations in noticing past patterns, stripped away unhealthy relationships, and is beginning to tap into who she really is, not who she became to please everyone else. It takes an immense amount of effort to do this.

For the caterpillar, transformation means disintegrating its old form to become "goop" while protected in a cocoon before emerging as a butterfly. You can imagine the energy required to do this, and it can't be very comfortable being formless and not able to see much, if it can see at all. It's not easy being goop!

Conscious or not of its eventual destiny, the old self, having served its purpose, is dying a type of death, and a natural grieving process occurs. In consoling my client about letting go of her past, I mentioned how Cher had a hard time because intellectually she grasped what was happening, but she became very upset when she realized the voice of her child was changing; her daughter was now becoming a son. And although the person she gave birth to was very much still there, she was losing Chastity in order to welcome Chaz.

Chaz Bono, and anyone who is transgender, has to deal with perhaps the most extreme of identity issues. The amount of courage it takes to make such a transition, especially in the public eye, is truly inspiring. Not only did Chaz have to know and be comfortable enough with himself to make such a seemingly drastic decision, but he also had the poise and confidence to articulate so graciously and effectively how and why he needed to do what he did, demonstrating a profound lesson for us all in ultimate self-awareness and love.

Chaz's story is an important and powerful one because no matter how we identify ourselves, we all go through various transformations throughout our lives—some more internal, others more external—in order to evolve into the best and fullest versions of our own humanity. His experience teaches us to be true to ourselves, accept and honor all of who we are, and trust that those who sincerely care for us will do so too, even if it does take some time to adjust. Chaz is more content in his new body and in his new life than he has ever been; the more of us who get to that place, the better off we all are.

Whether you want to find your voice, be more comfortable in your body, or express more of your Sal or Sally, start by creating a cocoon of support and a super-safe space as you peel back the layers and go through your transformation from goop to glorious, like a Butterfly![4]

Work It

July 12, 2011

Work is love made visible. And if you cannot work with love but only with distaste, it is better that you should leave your work and sit at the gate of the temple and take alms of those who work with joy. —Khalil Gibran

Years ago while watching *Project Runway*, I was very impressed by the then-unknown Christian Siriano, who as a finalist was preparing a collection for Fashion Week in his itty-bitty shoebox of an apartment that had room for only his sewing machine and creations. There was no furniture; he slept in a sleeping bag on the floor of the closet/hallway. Now a successful and respected designer because he lived, breathed and loved what he does, Christian surely found a way to "Make it work!"

Many of my clients in career transition find that this time is usually accompanied by or is a result of an identity crisis. Either their job consumed them so much that they forgot who they were, or their only sense of self came from the title and salary they received, and now that it's gone they are a bit lost, or they are not sure how they ended up doing what they were doing in the first place and don't want to do the same thing going forward.

Therefore, with unemployment at its highest in many years, we are reaching an epidemic proportion of people who are quite disoriented. *But*, the good news is that if you use this opportunity to do some internal work, you can really put yourself on the right track to the livelihood you were meant to have all along.

Much of what I do is help people discover that you are not your job. However, when you discover who you are, your labor is just a natural extension of yourself, of what you do, and of what you bring to this table of life. In other words, being employed and doing your work are two different things, which may or may not coincide at any particular time. The most important thing is to allow yourself to constantly evolve and do what you do, regardless of a paycheck or the environment.

For me, the only way I could exist was to make my employment and my work coincide. It's not a path for the faint of heart; it has been, and continues to be, a fascinating, challenging and thoroughly rewarding journey. But with all the ups and downs and unknowns, at the end of just about every day, I know I am doing my work, and the love of that work fuels every area of my life. This is the true American dream.

So this month, why not Show Me What You Got[5] with the ingenuity of Missy Elliott and the attitude of Snow White's dwarfs.[6] Finding a way to do the work that makes you feel most alive no matter what will help you create a life that is a pure labor of love!

New Rules

November 29, 2011

Rules are mostly made to be broken and are too often for the lazy to hide behind. —Douglas MacArthur

Hell, there are no rules here—we're trying to accomplish something. —Thomas Alva Edison

One of my all-time favorite films is *Strictly Ballroom* for a variety of reasons, one of which is how the main character, a world-class ballroom dancer, wants to use his own steps in competition and the outrage and, ultimately, the delight this causes. I've always loved to dance but hated formal exercise. Since I'm not out at the clubs much these days, Zumba and cardio salsa at the gym have filled the gap; but I was never into doing exactly what was presented—I generally stand in the back enjoying the music and *sort of* going along with the group.

I recently found a new class called Nia, which is perfect for me—it includes sections for "free dance" and encourages you to "dance it your way." It kind of looks like hippie dancing, or what you might do if you were in your room when no one was watching; it's a great workout that speaks to my body in a way that makes me feel good.

This time of year especially is filled with many traditions and routines, along with thoughts about the changes we want to make in the New Year. My mom has always made the holidays extra-special with borderline excessive (but not at all tacky) decorations around her home, and this year she just wasn't feeling it. When I suggested she could put up the tree with a few accent pieces instead of doing the whole Winter Wonderland/Santa's Workshop, she thought it was impossible—it had to be all or nothing.

I insisted it could be done and took some of the items she put in the same place every year and used them differently. She fought with me tooth and nail, until I proved they would indeed fit in spots she said they wouldn't. The house looks festive and the mission was accomplished; it feels like a maximum amount of decor with a minimal amount of effort! But it was her resistance to change and her incredulity that several options and alternatives existed that were the hardest parts to tackle—she simply couldn't see any way other than how she'd done it year after year.

Tradition can be a good thing, but it's important to know when those traditions and routines are serving or restricting us. Sometimes you just gotta break the rules, think out of the box, do it "your way." Where would we be without the hundreds and thousands of rule breakers, both known and unknown, in every field—especially the arts, science, fashion and civil rights?

But the truth is that often our most fervent rules and regulations have been totally self-imposed and/or are no longer necessary. It's easy to get caught up in doing the same old thing just because that's the way we've always done it. Sometimes we need a fresh eye, another brain, to look at the same situation and come up with a new solution, a new way of doing things that we couldn't see because we were too close or it was too engrained in our psyche.

Wondering if change will serve you better than reinforcing the "rules" you have in place right now, or which walls need to come Tumblin' Down[7] and be replaced with some new Moves Like Jagger?[8] Embrace your inner rebel and take the law into your own hands so you can create the right sequence of funky steps and dance to the beat of your own drum!

Sing Out Loud

December 6, 2011

I love to sing. I'm not very good, but I do it anyway. I have a "belting" playlist on my iPod and periodically sing my guts out for an audience of none; I keep my earphones on so I can't even hear my own off-pitch rendition. Sometimes I'll be walking down the street or sitting on a bench somewhere and sing slightly out loud, much to the amusement of passersby. Or I'll blast music in the car and sing at the top of my lungs, much to the dismay of my tween nephews who were with me recently during one such episode.

Singing releases pent-up energy and allows us to express emotions in a way that words without rhythm, harmony and melody simply cannot. The marriage of thoughts with a tune is a powerful, healing one and when done honestly and authentically, it can connect us to our deepest center, the very core of our being. As one of my favorite vocalists, Jill Scott, says, you can study music theory and employ various techniques, but when you come on stage "you gotta sing with your soul, play with your soul." Those who do are the performers who move us the most.

Like the Muppets and their friends, it's generally best to "Sing of good things, not bad / Sing of happy not sad,"[9] but songs can allow us to process darker feelings too ... just remember the purpose is to release and heal, not to get stuck and wallow.

You never need a reason to sing, but what better excuse to get your groove on than the holidays? There is no other time of year when it's more common and acceptable to round up some folks to do some caroling, or sit around the dining room table and sing a few festive tunes. Of course there's always karaoke, your bedroom mirror, or plenty of choirs and live acts if you need some extra inspiration.

Need a little push to exercise those vocal chords and activate your own personal *Glee*? Just start at the very beginning of your Do-Re-Mis[10] and find the song that helps you Dream On[11] so you can fa-la-la-la-la throughout this holiday season and beyond!

The Experiment

January 10, 2012

Life is not easy for any of us. But what of that? We must have perseverance and above all confidence in ourselves. We must believe that we are gifted for something, and that this thing, at whatever cost, must be attained.
—Marie Curie

Genius is 2 percent inspiration, 98 percent perspiration.
—Thomas Alva Edison

Marie Curie spent four grueling years in her laboratory without any guarantees that her work would not be in vain. As Albert Einstein commented, "The greatest scientific deed of her life—proving the existence of radioactive elements and isolating them—owes its accomplishment not merely to bold intuition but to a devotion and tenacity in execution under the most extreme hardships imaginable, such as the history of experimental science has not often witnessed."

As a result of her conviction, patience and fortitude, along with the support of her husband and partner, Pierre Curie, Marie Curie became the first woman to win a Nobel Prize and the first of only four people to have been bestowed the honor more than once!

It's important to note that the word *laboratory* contains the word *labor*, which means "to work." The word *experiment* derives from the same root as the word *experience*, which is defined as "practical contact with and observation of facts or events." In this great laboratory called Life, we are most alive and creative when stretching ourselves to make discoveries and determinations, or testing hypotheses of our own or others' making.

The only way for evolution and growth to take place is to step out of our comfort zones; to find what works and what doesn't, whether it be with health, career or relationships; and to find out what sticks and what is more suitable for the literal or metaphoric trash can. We must have a myriad of experiences—good, bad, and everything in between—because they are our best teachers. As I often tell my clients, "You need to get your hands dirty," to get out there, out of your bubble, out of the theory/fantasy in your head, and interact with life to see what it has in store for you, how it can mold and shape you, what you're made of, what your likes/dislikes are, and what new vistas it contains, all of which serve to make you ever stronger and wiser.

This is especially true when at a crossroads, a point of no return; when it seems you're at the edge of a cliff and the only option is to jump off to get to your next destination. As scary as that feels, the fear of moving forward is far better than the dread of staying where you are or turning back, knowing that failures, both big and small, will always beset you on this new journey in order to learn—like an infant who has to take those first steps, and fall many, many times, before it's able to walk confidently on its own. Remember that Edison never failed; he just found 10,000 ways that didn't work!

Just as the Founding Fathers called the formation of our nation the "greatest social experiment in history," which continues to have its share of successes and failures, this year why not commit to seeing your life, or at least one aspect of it, as your own experiment, with new actions based on sound information or solid intuition as knowledge is gained. Keep in mind and remember that some of us are more introverted so we need to explore more outwardly, and those of us who are more extroverted need to experiment with being quiet and exploring our internal worlds.

Need a little help with your personal or professional life research? Put on your lab coat and become the scientist who collects, analyzes and assesses the data you've accumulated so far, and take inventory of your inherent traits in order to discover (or rediscover) what will bring you the most fulfillment and success in 2012 and beyond!

Shake Your Groove Thing

November 28, 2012

Do you have the discipline to be a free spirit?
—Gabrielle Roth

In the movie *Silver Linings Playbook*, main characters Pat and Tiffany are in training for a big dance competition that turns out to be much more than a fancy booty-shaking contest. A unique romantic dramedy, it's a film that shows there is a fine line between sanity and insanity, and acceptable versus unacceptable behavior, and shows the beauty of living life to the beat of your own drum.

In the movie *The Sessions*, Mark O'Brien is confined to an iron lung 20 hours a day, existing on a gurney, unable to move from the neck down, and yet he writes poetry, is a professional journalist, and decides to hire a sex surrogate so he can experience the most human of experiences. We go along on his journey (based on a true story!) and find him to be one of the most alive, loving and liberated individuals to have ever lived, despite such extreme physical limitations.

And as seen in the movie *Lincoln*, our sixteenth president is clearly not your Average Joe. He was always thinking out of the box, using his quirky sense of humor to defuse or illuminate situations, and taking numerous risks throughout the most heart-wrenching circumstances our country has endured. He stretched the Constitution to its limit, working within an established framework while implementing his own interpretation and/or bending the rules based on hard-earned wisdom, keen observations, and superior judgement as unprecedented needs arose and critical decisions had to be made in order for progress to occur.

In the conscious movement class I take, we are told to "dance it your way," and we have breaks of "free dance" when we boogie as we see fit; it's not chaotic because there is an organized structure and unity within the flow as we come back together as a group intermittently throughout the hour. It's a super-small class because for many people, when given the opportunity to move and think for them-selves, even for just a few moments, it is a daunting and uncomfortable feeling; it's an empowering exercise that requires more effort and less inhibition, and many simply don't know what to do if they are not following an instructor. And that, my friends, is indicative of a larger problem, with implications reaching far beyond a gym studio.

Spielberg's Lincoln asks: "Can we choose to be born? Or are we fitted to the times we're born into?" As citizens of the 21st century, we are certainly living in extraordinary times that will require us to become the fullest and most unique beings we are meant to be. We each have something that needs to be expressed, something that no other person on this planet—no one who has come before or will come after—can express. Right now we need to find new ways of looking at old problems and change old ways in order deal with new problems, so it's more important than ever for people to do their own thang, because there is no other way to generate inspiration and give birth to innovation.

In any era, it's easy to get stuck in past habits and sucked into the zeitgeist of the day. Resist the urge to follow the herd, fight to honor yourself, think and speak your own thoughts, and begin to know yourself and create yourself anew every moment of every day—instead of being swept up by social media, news, commercials, and even your peer groups, work and ethnic cultures, or family and friends who are all, consciously or not, forces that can easily grab hold of your mind, body, spirit and/or bank account. Don't let your physical characteristics, family roots or societal dictates squash all the rhythms inside you that might be quite different from what those outside influences might have you believe, say or do.

Not sure exactly what your groove thing[12] is? Use some basic choreography to point yourself in the right direction, but ultimately You Should Be Dancing[13] your own steps throughout life, hopefully with a fun disco floor beneath your feet along the way!

Own It

February 4, 2014

Those of you who have known or worked with me for a while are aware that I have never been comfortable being the center of attention and am an introvert by nature. But I do have something to say and have been saying stuff in public now for many years!

As I mention in my seminars, Eleanor Roosevelt, one of my heroes, famously encouraged us to do the thing you fear the most. One of those things for me, besides being "on stage," is being in front of the camera. Another thing I talk about is that once you figure out who you are, own it. I'm also always saying that we teach what we need to learn (and write what we need to read), and since I do my best to walk my talk and practice what I preach ...

Last week I had someone videotape my seminar "Who Are You and What Are You Supposed to Be Doing With Your Life?" (an excerpt can be found on YouTube), which was attended by more than 70 people—putting me simultaneously on stage *and* in front a camera, and I thought I would own it and share it here. So what can *you* do today to own who you are?

Election

November 4, 2014

We are cursed with the blessing of consciousness and choice, a two-edged sword that both divides us and can help us become whole. ... The divided life may be endemic, but wholeness is always a choice. —Parker Palmer

In her appearance on OWN this past Sunday, spiritual thought leader and author Marianne Williamson, who recently ran for Congress but lost in the primary, said the higher purpose of democracy is that all people are "guaranteed the opportunity to self-actualize."

I was riveted by her comments at the end of the interview, because she was able to articulate so succinctly my philosophy about and understanding of this country, which I embody in my talks like "Who Are You and What Are You Supposed to Be Doing With Your Life?" and "Use Your Freedom to Create the Life of Your Dreams." It is why I have always believed in and loved being American, even if I haven't always been proud of it.

Regardless of what stage of growth our nation is in, the US is still a special place that allows us to become the highest and best versions of ourselves, the ease of which is tempered by varying degrees of circumstance, luck and justice. Not only can we elect our government representatives, but we can elect ourselves to run our own personal life race and make an infinite number of choices that enable us to be who we are meant to be due to a more palpable, if not literal, freedom than most, if not all, other countries on this planet.

But no matter where you are a citizen, we have more of a say in our lives than the external world of politics, religion and capitalism would have us (or want us to) believe. If you're honest with yourself, you'll realize that your life at this very moment is a culmination and sum total of every choice you've ever made. Depending on whether or not you like where you're at, meaning if you don't like it or want to make it even better, you can make different choices to result in a different direction.

If we summon the political will to use the power that really *is* in our hands, we can elect to react to any situation with love or fear, anger or compassion, understanding or hate. We can choose when and where to get involved outside of ourselves and make decisions that bring us either closer to or further from our authentic self and goals. I know where my vote goes!

We cast our internal ballot to either stew in a sea of what-ifs and shoulda coulda wouldas, or instead deal with the reality of what's in front of us as it stands, taking responsibility and appropriate action in order to plow forward and create a more favorable outcome. Try not to have any hanging chads here ...

We can choose our thoughts, making sure they are positive and expansive; we can acknowledge our feelings and allow ourselves to feel everything—good, bad or ugly—so we can govern them once we accept and learn from the awareness they are bringing to our attention. I've been campaigning for this for years!

In other words, we have the right to vote with our *consciousness* and use it accordingly, no matter what the circumstance. Make sure you are exercising this fundamental liberty in every area of your life—your work, your relationships, your health, and your community.

Need a little help getting comfortable with your own personal polling place? Be honest in toeing the party line of YOU, knowing that your victory will benefit a constituency that includes your family, friends, neighbors, and perhaps even the world!

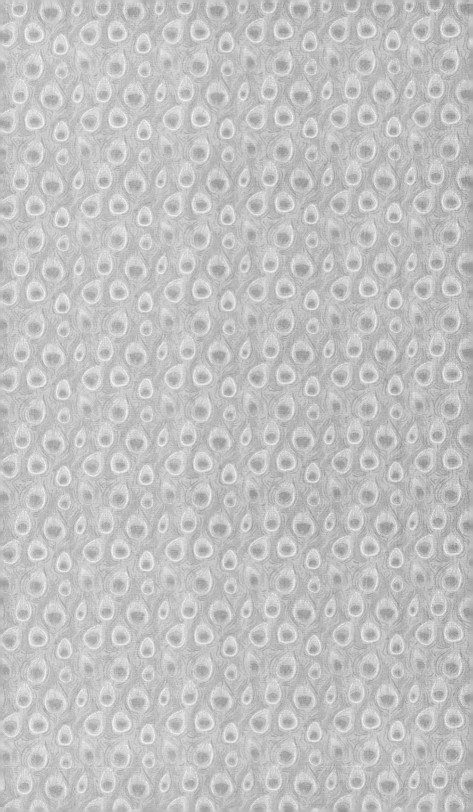

THE JOURNEY

Groundhog Day, the Grammys & Gaga

February 2, 2010

Today is Groundhog Day, and whether or not that furry creature sees its shadow, it marks the midpoint of winter— a time to be sure you've planted the seeds of all you want to bloom this Spring.

But today really reminds me of the fabulous movie starring Bill Murray, who wakes up over and over to the same day with a chance to make things right each time. He ultimately makes the best changes to himself and attracts Andie MacDowell, and they live happily ever after. It's a good time to reflect on what *you* are doing every day to help move closer to or further from your goals. As Einstein is often quoted as saying, "Insanity is doing the same thing over and over again and expecting a different result."

So what do the Grammys and Lady Gaga have to do with any of this? One year ago, you had probably never heard of her, yet on Sunday there she was, the opening act performing with Sir Elton John, on the biggest night in music. Overnight success? Never. From an early age, Gaga figured out who she was and what she was supposed to be doing with her life. And with a clear vision, talent and determination, she took steps every day to get there.

I don't know much about her journey, but one thing I will bet on is that it was INTENTIONAL, as everything about Gaga is. Anyone who was nominated or performed at the Grammys would have that in common, to varying degrees.

Wondering what success looks like for you? Take a little time to figure it out, and once you've identified it, use that clarity to find a way to get there. No matter what you want to do, make your life all about it morning, noon and night, and you'll see some amazing results day after day after day ...

Money Makes the World Go Round

March 2, 2010

Artists and musicians do it. Actors and writers do it. Designers do it. Nonprofits and entrepreneurs do it. To some extent, we all do it. We strive to maintain our authenticity, creativity and vision of who we are and what we want to express in the world while trying to earn a living in it.

I recently attended a lovely event hosted by In Good Company that highlighted the journey of fashion designer Selia Yang. She reinforced the idea that for successful creative types, not every decision can be 100 percent creative. To truly exist and thrive, you must understand and often defer to the financial/commercial aspects of life.

These types of especially dedicated lifestyles are the "roads less traveled" for a reason—if it was easy, everyone would be doing it! It's a path that takes faith, determination, perseverance and, perhaps most of all, courage.

The word courage has its root in the Latin word for heart. There is no doubt that to do what you want to do in life, you need lots of heart—in the form of love for yourself, others and your work—and the passion and conviction to forge ahead, even if you don't know for sure where your next meal will come from. This kind of courage arises not because of some great tragedy that has befallen you, but simply because of your integrity and commitment to that "creative" vision and life.

There's a reason it's called show business, and although nonprofits are not for profit, they still need money to do the work they do. In the past, we relied upon patrons and bene-factors, which to some extent we still do. The bottom line is that we need money to exist. How to achieve that balance of being who we are and being able to support ourselves is an eternal quest with no silver-bullet answer. At the end of the day, we need to be able to decide as individuals just how much we can compromise ourselves for it.

When choosing to live a life that is most true to who you are, you need to be aware of what you might have to sacrifice, at least for a while, to make things happen. But as challenging as the path can be, there is always a payoff for sticking with it—and we wouldn't have all the beauty, innovation, entertainment and opportunity in the world if others hadn't done so!

Still interested in walking down that path? You may have to redefine what success means to you. You need to possess certain traits along with the right motivation and perspective to know out how these choices will affect other areas of your life—but you will be more fulfilled for at least having tried.

Lost?

May 25, 2010

I never watched an episode of this much beloved recently departed TV series, but I learned that a lot of you out there have dedicated the past six-plus years to figuring out what it all means and wondering what you are going to do now that it's over.

Instead of trying to sort out what happened to the passengers of Oceanic Flight 815, why not spend as much time and energy making sense of the who, what, when, where and why of your own life, work and relationships, or even of the world. After all, fact is often stranger (and more interesting!) than fiction.

I'm always recommending that you spend more quality time with yourself, but a lack of hours in the day is often the excuse. So why not set aside at least half the time you devoted to watching, chatting about, and/or analyzing what was happening on the show—plus a little grace—and then, as the famous hymn[1] notes, if once you were lost, you can now be found. Amazing how that works!

But if you're feeling a little less than amazing or even blind, try to focus on how everything and everyone connects in your life and how you can make your personal season and series finale one to be proud of!

Steppin' Out

July 27, 2010

Last week marked the 41st anniversary of Apollo 11's landing on the moon, where the famous words uttered by Neil Armstrong beamed down, "That's one small step for man, one giant leap for mankind." You may never have your feet touch the lunar landscape, but can you imagine what kind of step would be the equivalent of that for your life here on Earth?

When you're on a tightrope or crossing a stream, you must be very conscious and super-present at every moment, because one wrong move would surely cause you harm. Each step serves its unique purpose to push you closer to your destination, no matter if there are 200, 20, or a very special 12.

As the wise saying goes, "A journey of a thousand miles begins with a single step." Sometimes we need to take baby steps, sometimes we have to take one giant step, and many times we feel as though we're taking one step forward and two steps back.

But most of all, it's important for us to step outside our comfort zone from time to time. If we don't take the initiative to stretch ourselves, then we often miss opportunities to learn and grow (although the Universe eventually ends up pushing us one way or another anyway)!

So if you are in transition or at a place where you feel your footing is a little unsure, you may need to reach out to someone who can help you get your bearings, hold your hand, keep you steady, and guide you along one step at a time—to get from one side of the riverbank to the other or from one moonbeam to the next.

Leap of Faith

October 12, 2010

In the year 1492, Columbus sailed the ocean blue. ... Whether or not we approve of the outcome of that fateful voyage of the Nina, Pinta and Santa Maria, we can all learn from Columbus's extreme act of faith and belief in himself when he left to explore a New World despite all odds.

Albert Einstein believed in intuition and inspiration, saying, "Imagination is more important than knowledge." The greatest discoveries in the world are often based on hunches by people with a vision and a certain knowingness, who then move forward with courage, determination and perseverance and set out to prove it. People may think you're crazy, want to dissuade you, say your theories are wrong; even those closest to you who have the very best of intentions can only project their version of the truth and what they think is right. But they simply may not understand, and at the end of the day, you must be the captain of your own ship.

Once you embark on that journey, you will always encounter stormy skies, dis-ease and potential mutiny, whether from external sources and naysayers, or internal voices of doubt and despair trying to capsize what your heart and gut know to be true. Your proof or evidence may not yet be in existence, but you must remain steady as she blows!

We each have an internal compass, our own North Star, which may very well lead us on a different path from everyone around us or society as a whole. We are all unique beings, so only *you* know what's right for you and ultimately the direction you want to be going. And if you're wrong or it doesn't work out the way you planned, at least you will have tried and will learn and grow along the way. You may even find something better than what you originally envisioned ...

Need a little adjustment to your internal GPS, an experienced cartographer, or just some help handling what Mother Nature throws your way? At the end of the day, you need to dig deep and become the wind that gives lift to your sails so you can navigate those uncharted waters and stay the course!

Going the Distance

November 9, 2010

The American poet and educator Henry Wadsworth Longfellow said, "Great is the art of beginning, but greater the art is of ending."

A marathon like the famous one NYC just held is a fantastic metaphor for life and how to accomplish what you want. It begins with a commitment, after which you must prepare and discipline yourself with dedication and enthusiasm. You must travel lean—lighten your load of physical, mental and/or emotional baggage along the way. There will be moments when you feel you can't go on, but someone, even a complete stranger, will say or do something that will spur and cheer you on. You must have faith in yourself and know there is indeed light at the end of the tunnel.

I have a client who, after being laid off from his corporate job, realized he wanted to run his own business to be more in control of his future. With a deep belief in himself and a lot of trial and error, blood, sweat and tears, a year and a half later he is now a top national producer. He keeps his eye on the prize, paces himself, and with stamina and persistence is able to get the job done (and continues to attend our weekly Thursdays at Three group to stay on track, stay balanced, and gain support!).

Even with the uncertainty that owning a business brings, he is infinitely happier than when he was working 9 to 5 with a steady paycheck. Because he knew what he wanted, made the internal decision, and took the necessary external steps, he now reaps the immediate and tangible results of his efforts.

Whether a tortoise or a hare, slow and steady generally wins the race, no matter how long it takes. As long as you *start* and *finish* it, there is satisfaction because the journey is just as significant, if not more so, than the goal. The important thing is not to compare yourself to others—because we are all at different places in this marathon called life; you need to know what your personal best is in whatever area you are focusing on.

No one can run that race for you, but whether beginner or pro, you need to aim for the most direct and satisfying route to the finish line, accepting guidance, cheers and some motivational Gatorade every step of the way!

The Price Is Right?

April 12, 2011

Last week I saw the Broadway revival *Born Yesterday*. The show, which was made into a movie classic in 1950, could not be more timely with its themes of corporate and government greed, the corruption between the two, and the price one is willing to pay for a glamorous life in lieu of an honorable one.

I also recently attended a seminar on negotiation, in which the very credentialed professor asked us to assign monetary values to almost everything we do in order to reach an optimal decision for any situation, e.g., leaving our significant other for an opportunity, or moving to an undesirable location for a job. I found the exercise to be an interesting one that I didn't totally agree with, but the point he was trying to make is that everyone has their price.

When the government narrowly avoided a shutdown over budget issues, there was much back-and-forth about which party was going to concede what to keep our country functioning. In these times of uncertainty, especially if you are in career transition, you must ask yourself: What am I willing to sacrifice in order to get what I want and make ends meet?

The world must transform its values from profit to purpose, and it's up to us to demand it. Traditionally our culture has made such a transformation difficult, and in some ways it's getting more so. On the other hand, things are beginning to change as people become more unsatisfied and search for a life of meaning, while corporations are responding to consumers' desire for their dollars to do double duty via cause-related marketing, corporate social-responsibility initiatives, and social entrepreneurship in general.

The tide is *slowly* turning, but in the meantime you may feel caught between a rock and a hard place trying to do something in line with your authentic self that earns a decent living. But if you are in a job only for the paycheck, you might want to analyze what being in that position is costing your health, your relationships, and your peace of mind. Just as everyone has a price, everything comes with a price.

The ultimate goal is to have a prosperous life that comes from a place of principles and to have quality over quantity; the two do not have to be mutually exclusive, but it is a journey that requires commitment, time and patience.

We all have a little Material Girl[2] or guy in us, but there's no reason to become any version of Lady Marmalade,[3] Roxanne,[4] or Just a Gigolo.[5] So [your name here], "Come on down!" and discover how your goods can serve others *and* you without selling out, and create a win-win situation in every area of your life.

An Apple for the Teacher

September 6, 2011

I am not a teacher, but an awakener. —Robert Frost

The dream begins, most of the time, with a teacher who believes in you, who tugs and pushes and leads you on to the next plateau, sometimes poking you with a sharp stick called truth. —Dan Rather

Better than a thousand days of diligent study is one day with a great teacher. —Japanese proverb

It's that time of year when notebooks and knapsacks abound and all sorts of new beginnings and nerves are in the air, bringing the possibilities and excitement that arrive with the start of an academic year. Whether or not we find ourselves in an actual classroom this fall, we are all students in this school called Life, which means that anyone and any situation can be our teacher, and education can come in all shapes and forms.

It is often those who are closest to us who teach us the exact lessons we never knew we needed (or wanted) to learn—either directly, like my 6-year-old niece, who in her own words very calmly told my brother she wished he hadn't found the prescription sunglasses he'd lost for the umpteenth time because he needed to learn to pay better attention to his personal possessions and the harsher consequences of their non-recovery; or indirectly, like a co-worker, friend or family member who likes to talk a lot and forces you to be a better listener, have more patience, and/or set boundaries.

Whatever "class" you are in, sometimes you must first fail miserably in order to then pass with flying colors, because you can't learn anything without making a few mistakes, a little trial and error to perfect that which you need to master ... Hopefully you can figure out that the experience itself was the teacher, or have someone around to help you glean what you need to learn, and grow as a result. The good news is that you will never repeat a "class" when you've truly learned a lesson the hard way, and if you're lucky, sometimes you can even have a teacher who helps you skip several grades.

Whether you think like Pink Floyd[6] or feel like Lauryn Hill,[7] learning is a lifelong process and everything serves its purpose in the bigger picture for you to graduate at the end of your life with honors.

So this September, be grateful for all those amazing teachers you've had both inside the classroom and out. Thank the role models, mentors and instructors who serve as great examples of achievement and inspiration, as well as the challenging bosses, employees and clients, the bullies and mean girls, the tough coach, your current or ex-boyfriend/girlfriend/partner/spouse, your pain-in-the-neck big or little brother/sister, anyone who ever gave you a hard time, and especially those difficult "tests" you endured, because they too helped form your character and are all opportunities to make you a better you.

Need to repeat (or stop repeating) a few classes to bring you closer to the grade you deserve? A little tutoring or outside perspective can help make sure you get a gold star or A-plus on that project, because you can make your life much closer to a 4.0 than you could ever imagine!

What's Your Number?

October 4, 2011

Age is all imagination. Ignore years and they will ignore you.
—Ella Wheeler Wilcox

I'm one of those people who can't remember how old she is. Because 1.) it's irrelevant and 2.) I honestly feel like I'm 25 (I'm not). I believe this is the main reason others often assume I am much younger than my birth certificate would state, and I recently came across a greeting card that perfectly expressed this phenomenon. It read, "How old would you be if you didn't know how old you were?"

I like to think of myself as ageless and timeless, but my brain will do a double take every now and then when I find out the numbers of people around me (who I tend to think are the same age as when I originally met them, even though 14 years have passed) or when I hear that famous folks like Beyonce, Britney, Paris and Justin are all turning 30 this year, and about Sting, who just turned 60!?! But then again, 60 is the new 40 ...

Then there's my Mom, who will be celebrating her 66th revolution around the sun next week, but who has been experiencing the adolescence and early adulthood she never had, which began a few years after becoming single again at age 51 when my father passed away. She is out at her clubs most Friday, Saturday AND Sunday nights, dancing and flirting into the wee hours of the morning. She does online dating (several sites), has oodles of admirers (many younger than her) and a gang of giggly girlfriends (mostly around her age) to have fun with and gossip about it all. Really, I'm not exaggerating. My friends are in awe.

I was recently invited to two fancy shindigs honoring and almost exclusively attended by men and women in their "third acts." It made me reflect on how I've lived my life so far, and it reminded me that vitality at any age is always about how you take care of and feel about yourself, and it reinforced my trademark admonishment to make the most of the time and energy you have while you have it.

Abraham Lincoln is often quoted as saying, "And in the end, it's not the years in your life that count. It's the life in your years." So I say who cares about the number?! Just embrace wherever you're at and let your enthusiasm for living make you glow. And if you feel you haven't been getting the best bang for your mind, body and spirit's buck, then simply start to make the most of the years you still have, no matter how many you've already left behind!

Life Is Like a
Box of Chocolates

June 20, 2013

I often feel like Forrest Gump, bearing witness to the personal history of many interesting and notable folks, serendipitously finding myself in significant places at precisely poignant moments.

Nine years ago at a fundraising event, I was present for one such moment, when Kirsten Gillibrand turned to me and said, "I think I'm going to run for Congress" as I stood at the bar next to, of all people, Andrew Cuomo (between jobs at the time, now New York's governor) and Moby. Who could have imagined then that not only would she become a US senator only four years later in a fluke appointment, but that she would rise well above the challenge and take actions so bold that she would be catapulted onto the national stage. Watching her fight for justice for victims of sexual assault in the military, among her other numerous accomplishments, has been inspiring, to say the least.

Seven years ago I was at a small book party where a then-largely-unknown Dr. Oz was speaking to me and another woman about holistic women's healthcare, which is her area of expertise. Little did I know the phenomenon he would become, eventually having his own TV show, and that she would publish a book that was recently featured on that program, with her as a guest!

About six years ago I had the opportunity to travel with and spend some time getting to learn about noted religious scholar and author Karen Armstrong. I was blown away by her ability to articulate the unity and compassion of all religions, something our world so desperately needs to grasp. I couldn't believe she hadn't been on *Oprah* and felt so strongly about it that I went on and on to her about how "we" needed to get her on there. Although I had nothing to do with it, I couldn't have been more thrilled to see that she was recently featured on OWN's *Super Soul Sunday*, which is an even better format for her, and one where she should return.

Then there is one of my clients whom I met with five years ago because she was miserable and hating her job, and whose dream was to become a Broadway producer; after a few years she did indeed become one, and she just won a Tony Award for best musical.

There are many, many other stories I could tell you, like the time I was crossing a street on September 11, 2008, just when a van carrying then-*candidate* Obama was driving by and he was stopped at a light right in front of me. Or when I just happened to be walking down the block when the Dalai Lama was walking out of his hotel. Or just the other day, when I nearly tripped over a man who was then introduced to me as Peter Diamandis, founder of XPRIZE Foundation, whose mission is to help bring about "radical breakthroughs for the benefit of humanity."

What it all means I really can't say, but I do know it's happened too many times for me not to pay attention, and it reminds us that we are each a part of living history—because today's events and everyday people could be tomorrow's milestones and leaders—and that every person has a journey, and to bear witness to that journey is an honor and makes very real and tangible the possibility of what anyone can achieve over time.

What surprises are around the corner or in your next bite? If you open yourself up to the biggest possibilities of *your* life, you can experience the magic that can happen when you follow your heart, live in the present, and have faith that the Universe will guide you to the right people and the right places at the right time. And that's all I have to say about that.

Whoa, Nelly

January 28, 2014

We don't want to hear about the process because we want everything to be instantaneous. Process in life always comes before the promotion. —T.D. Jakes

Now so much I know that things just don't grow if you don't bless them with your patience.[8] —First Aid Kit

As I am in the midst of my seventh year of coaching professionally, I find this a major theme that comes up over and over with most everyone I work with. Everybody wants answers and results overnight; they want action steps and bullet points to go from A to B to C. And they get very frustrated when I tell them it doesn't work like that!

But if they listen, do the "homework," and begin to understand and internalize what I have to say, it is inevitable that they will get answers, rediscover and connect to themselves, see light at the end of the tunnel, feel an inner shift, gain a new perspective, land their dream job, increase their self-esteem, and are more integrated and fulfilled than they could have ever imagined. And more times than not, at the end of the day, month, year(s), I get a begrudging ... "You were right!"

For any lasting growth and change to occur, you have to embrace the three Ps—process, patience and persistence. Depending upon what you are working on, you could see or feel results after one session, six weeks, six months, or three years; some shifts are big and external, but most are subtle and more internal because they are still "cooking." Remember we are always evolving, and the acorn does not become the oak tree overnight!

Certain times of the year inspire more focus on change than others, whether organic or collectively agreed upon with, say, a Western calendar. Do the resolutions you made January 1 already feel long gone or like a false start? The good news is that you have a second chance in a few days with the Lunar New Year, which I've always felt was more accurate since, as humans, we are more in harmony with the cycles of the moon ...

This will be the Year of the Horse, so before you go galloping into the future all willy-nilly, be sure you are implementing the changes that you *truly* desire and are going in the best direction at this time in your life, or perhaps you need a course correction. Either way, you want to harness that energy to make the most of the months ahead. By doing that, you, like the Horse Whisperer, can be the guide to the clarity, balance and direction you need in every area of your life to make 2014 your best calendar *and* lunar year yet! Gong Xi Fa Zai!

Vision Quest

April 8, 2014

When the Universe speaks, I listen. Not in a burning-bush-on-a-mountain kind of way, but through some combination of random Facebook postings, TV shows/commercials, signs both literal and figurative, and people known and unknown. Always repetitive.

In fact, most of the time I try to think as little as possible and instead pay very close attention to the world within and around me to get the answers/direction I need. I find that the best information we have often exists in this 3-D experiential form more so than in the gray matter between our ears, and that there is much wisdom in receiving and perceiving what comes our way. (Plus it's more fun and takes less effort to operate like this!)

Anyway, after the stock market crashed, "it" hinted to me in several ways that I should start some sort of group thing; when a third person point-blank raised his hand in my breakout session at an NYU symposium for laid-off financial professionals and asked, "Can you put a group together?" I could no longer ignore the request. So exactly five years ago this month, Thursdays at Three was born and has been going strong without a break ever since—first weekly after-noons during the height of the recession, then eventually bimonthly, with an evening session called Tuesday Talk for folks who had found employment but asked to continue with coaching and support, or for others who wanted to make a career change or simply manage their work and life better.

It's been quite the journey—and one of the most rewarding and important things I've done to grow both personally and professionally. It has made me a far better coach and facilitator, so thank you to all who have participated, especially those four brave souls who ventured out and trusted me that first day!

As many of you know, my path has been a long and varied one. In January 2001 I founded a nonprofit organization called The Women's Mosaic (TWM) after a lot of soul-searching and the result of a random workshop I picked from a Learning Annex catalog and attended out of sheer desperation four months earlier. Among other things, that workshop was exactly what I needed to confirm and crystallize an idea that was floating around in my s ubconscious—and 13 years, 100 events, a coaching and speaking career later, the rest is history!

Of course when I told people how I started TWM, they all wanted to do the same kind of workshop, so we began offering it twice a year with amazing and profound results, attracting many repeat attendees with incredible stories throughout. The last one was in September 2012 and had been on indefinite hiatus since for various reasons. But in the past month, after various signs and in combo with not one, not two, but *three people* within a few weeks asking me when we were doing another, I knew it was time—which means that many of you out there need this experience and it's no coincidence that you are reading this right now!

Visioning workshop or not, you don't need some shamanic ceremony or '80s movie to help you decide. Just listen to your Self, pay attention to the signs, and heed the call to make some big changes in your life—this is simply a way to fast-track the process!

Life Class

April 30, 2014

My first job out of college was teaching Spanish for grades 7-11 at a private school in New Jersey. I started right before I turned 22. I left way before I turned 23.

Fast-forward many, many moons and this past month I found myself in a high school classroom again, this time in a NYC public school's ninth grade to talk about social media.

Don't ask. Those of you who know me will find this laughable since I am a recovering technophobe who probably wouldn't even be online if I didn't kinda have to be for my type of work.

It all happened very quickly—I was asked on a Wednesday if I would start the first of six classes the following Monday, and without much thinking said yes, I guess because I trusted the person and wanted to see if I could now handle the critters who gave me so much grief way back when. Besides, I've been speaking/teaching for years, and I remember ninth grade being my favorite at the time, so why not? Social media? Apparently the entire curriculum would be provided; I just had to deliver it.

HAH! After the first day, with little to no preparation or training, it was like being thrown into a tank with 40 cranky sharks—what did I get myself into?!?! I held my own, but nearly quit. Other days it was like wrangling cats. But there were a few days of pure magic.

After surveying the students and finding out they spend nearly 100 percent of their free time on social media, I realized that a.) that's the first problem, and b.) beyond the general predator and online reputation issues (along with their celebrity obsession), when looked at through the lens of cyberbullying and the associated psychological and physical tolls—as in murders and suicides—it quickly occurred to me that having them understand the proper and positive use of social media, texting and the Internet could not be a more important and serious assignment ... and that it was quite literally a matter of life or death. In other words, I realized that since they live most of their lives on social media, I was really there to teach them about life.

Aha! Now *that* made sense, because that is what I do for my day job. Let's just say I tweaked the lesson plans I was provided.

It was an eye-opening experience to say the least. I could go on telling you how much I learned about kids, education, their future, our future, and the culpability of adults; the upsetting things I discovered about how our youth behave, what they think, and what they do to each other; how they only care about being famous; how I tried in our short time together to turn some of those things upside down and instill them with completely new empowering ideas and perspectives (yes, the Golden Rule was one of the "new" concepts introduced after you could hear crickets when I asked if anyone could tell me what it was); and how I held their attention with my knowledge of Justin Bieber. (Yes, I saw *Never Say Never* and was impressed—don't laugh—it was relevant because of how he used YouTube to become famous, but he is/was extremely talented and worked hard even though he's had some trouble lately ... not to mention second-highest amount of followers on Twitter, etc.)

I know this is probably the first and only time some of these kids will hear about such things, and I'm pretty sure I reached at least a few who will now think a little differently about their lives and the consequences of their actions, both online and off. But I know for sure there was at least one who truly got it.

After the third lesson, which was the first on cyberbullying and the aforementioned wrangling cats day, I was caught off guard when after class, a soft-spoken but confident kid from the back of the room came up to me, shook my hand and said, "Miss, I just wanna let you know I really appreciate you." He had me at appreciate! But he went on to say how disgusted he was with his classmates, that they weren't taking this seriously and that he had been listening to a lot of Bob Marley lately and was looking for his purpose, how he wanted to be a leader and that today he found his calling. STOP THE PRESSES. "Purpose" and "calling" were the exact words he used. I cannot make this up. And you can imagine to some-one who does a talk called "Who Are You and What Are You Supposed to Be Doing with Your Life?" it was like winning the lottery.

My work was done (or as my new colleague Karim goes, "Boom!" while gesturing the dropping of a mic and exiting stage left), even if no one else got it and did not listen to the next three lessons!

Junior and I talked about how he might accomplish such a mission, and I asked if he would like to start by talking to the class. Our final day together he did just that—the first time he had ever spoken in front of a room! And he was an unlikely candidate to do so according to him and his teachers, who say he's not a great student, and he admittedly wasn't even the best kid but had recently had a change of heart—and my class helped to solidify and confirm his new direction. With no coaching from anyone, he spoke for almost 15 minutes about how his peers need to wake up and take life and education "fa real" and do something that helps others. I couldn't have been more inspired and proud, as I know for anyone, especially at that age, to get up in such an environment and speak his truth was quite remarkable. It was one of the best days of my life.

I tell you all this because I did not do anything special—all I did was *listen to my gut, show up, be myself and do my thing*, which is all you can ever do, regardless of the context. You never know what the bigger plan is and how affecting *just one person* can make a huge difference. The Universe knows what it's doing—and what it had to do to get me in the same room with that 14-year-old black boy was nothing short of a miracle.

Still not a Belieber? Whether you're 15 or 51, you're never too young or too old to take responsibility for your life, discover who you are, and be confident enough to share it with the world, 'cause it takes more than just a #Selfie[9] to have a positive impact in the Twitterverse and beyond ...

SELF-LOVE & CARE

Discipline Is Not a Dirty Word

February 23, 2010

Whether it makes you think of Catholic school nuns, dog training, or your struggle with diet and exercise, discipline— of the mind and body—is what we are certainly witnessing as we watch the Winter Olympics. Any form of excellence requires it, and these amazing athletes show what can happen when a person is singularly focused on and dedicated to a particular goal.

I admit that for most of my life, I associated the word with limitation—something negative, bad or oppressive. Over the past several years I have learned that instead, discipline is a positive attitude and approach that can actually be quite liberating. When used in the right way, it is an extreme act of self-love.

For example, realizing that I needed to stop working 24/7 and make time for activities that are fun, pleasurable and social is something I am now very conscious about. I even include going to the gym in that category! It has become a discipline of mine that has made my life a lot less stressful and more enjoyable.

As they say, "One man's pleasure is another man's pain"— and I say what you may consider a pain for yourself can often turn into a pleasure once you discipline yourself in that area and reap the benefits!

Discipline means you care so deeply about yourself that you want to improve or create balance wherever you need it. No matter what goals you are working toward, you are doing something every day to make yourself the best you can be.

But sometimes we can't do it alone. Like those Olympic athletes, who are able to stay on that razor-edge track with the help of their coaches, receiving guidance and support can bring you a personal gold medal in whatever area of life you choose!

Tiptoe Through the Tulips

April 13, 2010

Spring has finally sprung! Everywhere you look, flowers and trees are blooming up a storm—the colorful symphony of tulips, lilacs, daffodils, cherry blossoms and dogwoods are waking up the city from its cold, long winter slumber, filling us with gorgeous eye candy and reminding us of the new possibilities that exist within and around us.

It's such a fleeting moment; it seems to last only a week or two, so it's now or never to take notice and appreciate the beauty and magic while it exists. This is a perfect time to pay attention to the prettiest new little things around you, and to celebrate these glorious gifts of Nature.

Beauty is one of the greatest pleasures in life, and a flower is one of the simplest and most tangible expressions of it. If you can't soak up everything that is staring you in the face right now, then how will you recognize and appreciate the more subtle beauty within and around you throughout the year?

In New York City we tend to rush from here to there, with our noses in our BlackBerrys or with blinders on as we think about whatever, when what we really need to do in those transitional times throughout the day is stop and smell the roses, literally and figuratively. Slowing down, taking a few deep breaths and becoming aware of our surroundings, especially when they are so lovely, is a great cure for stress and anxiety. I'm sure that if you just try it, like Mikey, you'll like it!

Feeling a little curmudgeonly with all this zip-a-dee-doo-dah[1] talk? Try spending some time enjoying the season so you can re-energize and help get things goin' your way again.

Smile in Your Liver

May 4, 2010

In the best-selling book *Eat, Pray, Love*, author Elizabeth Gilbert visits a holy man in Bali who gives her a meditation to smile in every part of her body, "Even in your liver." This is a great way to activate the feelings of joy within. Just reading that makes you feel a little lighter and more relaxed, doesn't it?

Well if that doesn't do it, then what will? Whatever the thought or image is, make sure you get a daily dose in order to keep yourself young, happy and at peace. Doing so has numerous health benefits, and when identified and used properly, it is cheaper and better than any diet pill, drug or food out there!

Whether savoring a scoop of gelato, relishing in a job well done, experiencing a romantic moment, or watching an episode of *Glee*, recognize and cherish those moments when you feel joyful. Try to sustain and bathe in those sensations for as long as you can and be able to recall them when you need them most.

I recently attended a friend's musical, and for an hour and a half it had me smiling from ear to ear and from my heart, gut and yes, even my liver. If he had not followed his calling to create, I would not have enjoyed the positive mental, physical and emotional benefits that came along with it.

Everyone has the capacity to bring joy to the world, or at least to someone else. So take the time to figure out what your joy is because when you do, it will be your pleasure to bring it to the world—and others' pleasure to receive it.

The Pleasure Principle

August 3, 2010

A client of mine recently had a job interview and the first question posed to her was, "So what do you do for fun?" Caught off guard like a deer in headlights, she searched the cobwebs of her memory to come up with something from the last decade.

I often advise folks to relax and take time off, and I have to convince them that a healthy dose of pleasure is indeed productive. When I suggest that they do something that's a treat for them, an automatic excuse is that they "can't afford it," but there are many things you can do that don't cost a lot of time or money.

You can find joy and relaxation in simple pleasures like listening to your favorite music, taking a Zumba class, playing bridge, laughing with a good friend, cooking a delicious meal, being on the beach at sunset or sunrise, taking a walk at lunchtime, riding a roller coaster, drinking a cold beer on a hot summer day, cuddling with your pet, reading a good/trashy novel or fashion/tabloid magazine, or enjoying the swirly goodness of Pinkberry made extra-special by half-off happy-hour prices!

And don't forget, our bodies are built for pleasure, so be sure to make time for that too, and reap the scientifically proven benefits that accompany a good roll in the hay with that special someone in person, or in your head ... (Javier Bardem anyone?)

All work and no play, or too much play and not enough work, will most definitely *not* keep the doctor away. As in all things, balance and awareness are key. Taking a few moments, hours and days to adjust on a regular basis will make your life more refreshed, energized and focused—and contribute to landing that next job!

So if the last time you remember having fun coincided with Janet Jackson's 1986 hit song,[2] or you can't seem to allow yourself to let go every now and then, give yourself the permission you need to put the pep back in your step and the zest back in your quest!

High Anxiety

December 7, 2010

This time of year, with its emphasis on excessive merry-making and gift-giving, combined with cold weather, shorter days, and a challenging economy (and this year, with Mercury in retrograde thrown in!) would cause even the jolliest of Santas to pack his sled and head back to the North Pole to hibernate the way his grizzly neighbors so wisely do.

Our focus is on parties and socializing, yet our natural tendency is to go inward for the winter; we are pulled to do all these external things in a very short amount of time when we should be winding down and checking in with ourselves and preparing for the New Year. As a result, we find ourselves off balance in a big way. It's no wonder anxiety and stress levels skyrocket and we just try to do our best not to crack under the pressure of the ho-ho-ho!

So how to make it through the holidaze intact? We need to be extra-mindful, stay centered and connected to ourselves, and not go to extremes or make any major decisions. Have an extra dose of patience with yourself and others; take deep breaths; laugh it off; do lots of yoga, tai chi and meditation; use Rescue Remedy; have a massage; make soup; get some fresh air; spend quality time with good friends; cuddle with your loved ones; and most of all, be kind and gentle to yourself.

Another idea is to give yourself the gift of spending time with someone, perhaps even me, who can offer an unbiased, positive perspective; someone who will put you back on track and in balance wherever you need it. Being able to identify what's going on in your head and ridding yourself of whatever is ho-ho-holding you back will enable you to enjoy a truly peaceful and joyous holiday season!

Lighten Up

December 21, 2010

Last night we experienced a rare occurrence of the Winter Solstice and a total lunar eclipse overlapping; this means the shortest day of the year combined with the cover-up of a full moon to give us a double dose of darkness. Although there is some debate and lots of myths about what effects these sorts of things have on people, after the year—and especially past couple of months—we've had, my interpretation is that "it's always darkest before dawn."

The good news is that the days will now be getting progressively longer and bright. It's important at this time of year to take in all the literal sunlight you can. Think of the rays as vitamins for your mind, body, spirit and soul, a lack of which can alter your moods, as anyone with SAD will attest. It's also a good idea to keep things as "light" as possible—do a little dancing (even if it's just around the house) or Zumba, and be sure to laugh a lot. At the very least, you will make others smile when they see you sunbathing in 29-degree weather!

As we approach the end of the year, it's also a good time to shed some light on what you've accomplished this past year. Many of my clients are in career transition, so it's easy for them to feel as if nothing has happened; or if you are just going about your business from day to day, it's easy to lose track of what has actually transpired over the past 12 months.

So make sure you take at least a couple of hours with your journal and calendar to jog your memory and see what external things you experienced and accomplished this year, big or small. Then let them help you recall how you have grown and what has changed for you internally. What mental and/or emotional shifts have occurred, in terms of your perceptions of yourself, your life, your work, and your relationships? How have they affected some of the external actions you took or that happened to you?

Having a little trouble seeing the proof in the pudding of how far you've come along? Perhaps an outside objective point of view from a trusted friend, mentor or coach (perhaps even me) can help push you to see where you've been and where you want to go, lighting the way to a more peaceful and prosperous new you!

Note: This was my last original Personal Growth Gab post of the year—who knew that I would be disciplined enough to write every week (50 out of 52 weeks!)—and that people would actually read them?! It's one of my best accomplishments of 2010.

Chillax

May 31, 2011

Twenty-first-century guru Deepak Chopra tells us, "Relaxation is the prerequisite for that inner expansion that allows a person to express the source of inspiration and joy within." He seems like one chill and content dude to me, so he must be on to something!

With the lazy, hazy days (i.e., hot and humid in NYC) that arrive with the unofficial start of summer comes a natural slowing down that also includes an increase in time spent outdoors, at the beach, in a park or in the country, which is especially important for us city slickers. As a great ad by the Bronx Zoo reminds us: Connecting with Nature. There's no app for that.

If, like many of my clients, you're someone who tends to go, go, go and give, give, give and feel as if every minute of every day needs to be "productive," you may have a difficult time adjusting to this slower pace and doing things that are *seemingly* frivolous and serve no purpose. But it's essential to have a balance of both kinds of activities in order to grow and heal, because it's in the relaxing that we are able to receive—whether a thought/idea/solution, love and affection that someone is offering us, or the love that we give ourselves by doing something healthy that we enjoy and feels good.

This summer, why not make it a goal to power nap at least once a day, breathe, check in with yourself periodically, write in a journal, listen to your favorite tunes, lose yourself in a good book, and savor the space between the tweets. Give yourself a TV and Facebook fast; cook delicious meals with produce from a farmer's market. The idea is to use this season to learn the discipline of relaxing and taking pleasure in simple things, which gives you room to grow. And then you can take your new habits into a more daily routine year-round ...

So if you're having a hard time going from 60, 70 or 80 miles an hour to 20, 10 or even zero, force yourself to put on the brakes, linger in the leisure, move to the groove, and have some Hot Fun in the Summertime![3]

One Is the Magic Number

November 8, 2011

There's just me. —Jill Scott

The number one has always garnered a lot of attention. With all that talk about "the one percent," who came in first place, and what gets to be No. 1 on which list, it should be no surprise there has been lots of hoopla about last week's date, 11-1-11, and even more for this Friday, 11-11-11.

It takes only one person to change the world (for good or bad), and whether conscious of it or not, we all strive to have those blissful moments of becoming one with something or someone outside ourselves. It can happen with your loved ones but also with your dance partner, your paintbrush, your horse, your golf club, your violin, Nature or the whole of humanity.

You also need to take care of number one, because if you don't, who will? How can you help anyone else if you haven't first cared for yourself? And hey, if *you're* happy, there's a much greater chance everyone around you will be happy too, like the proverbial pebble thrown in a pond whose ripples go out far beyond …

One doesn't have to be the Loneliest Number,[4] because at the end of the day you're the only one you've got—no one else can inhabit your body, mind and spirit, or experience your challenges and successes. You are ultimately responsible for your own joy and fulfillment, and how you relate to the world and make the most of what you've been given.

You only have One Life to Live, so how can you know and love who you are and what you think, feel and desire if you don't spend some quality time with yourself on a regular basis?

The proverb tells us, "A journey of a thousand miles begins with a single step," so now is as potent a time as any to finally make some effort, take some action toward a goal or way of being that you want to achieve, and/or be open to discovering new, unimagined opportunities and vistas that may bring you out of your comfort zone but closer to your best life.

As Bono sings, we're One,[5] but we're not the same, we've got to carry each other, so you might need an outside perspective to help you see there's just One in a Million You,[6] focus on who should be Numero Uno[7] in your life right now, and move toward feeling One Love[8] more than ever!

Roots

February 6, 2013

With the current release of films like *Lincoln* and *Django Unchained*, and with BET bringing the acclaimed '70s TV series *Roots* out of the vault, there's been a spotlight on and discussion about this essential part of our nation's history both on screen and off.

Whether or not you are a direct descendant of someone who lived or worked on a plantation in the 19th century, all of us in the 21st century, no matter who or where we came from, can check in to see which areas of our lives need to be emancipated from the tyranny of whatever is keeping us down, holding us back, or making us feel "less than" in both subtle and overt ways.

Oprah expressed it perfectly when she called slavery "a machine to create inferiority." You can only imagine what amazing strength, utter self-belief, and profound self-worth was required to break out of that mentality, to *really* know who you are and be able to simply exist, let alone thrive, despite others' perceiving you and often treating you in, well, let's just say a most unfavorable way. The fortitude it would take to preserve and protect yourself, your spirit, and your soul under such circumstances is almost beyond comprehension.

We certainly continue to struggle in a variety of ways with the legacy and repercussions of slavery in terms of race, while at the same time have come very far. But regardless of the color of our skin, there are more inconspicuous ways that we are judged—much of which has to do with what we think of ourselves when we look in the mirror, are alone with our thoughts, and by the choices we make in every area of our lives.

The foundation of who we are reaches far and wide throughout our work, relationships, health and everyday life, so the stronger and deeper your tree grows, the more you can weather even a storm like Sandy. Yes, you might lose a few branches along the way, but you won't be knocked out for good! So take some time this month to connect to the root of who you are, using this last part of winter to develop, heal, and love yourself so you can blossom more fully come Spring.

You might have some family roots to dig up or some grass roots to build up in the process, but the bottom line is that if you look at any problem, challenge or change you want to make and trace it back to its ultimate root—if you're honest with yourself—you will find that the buck stops with you.

Remember this is always good news, because that means *you* can do something about it. You can trace all the literal and metaphorical genealogical dots of your life and career to the root of the matter, and when you do, just like Alex Haley and Kunta Kinte in Africa, you can shout, "I found you!"

A Body at Rest

February 20, 2013

Newton's famous law states that a body at rest stays at rest and a body in motion will stay in motion until some external force acts upon it. With our 24/7, always-on, hyperconnected, overachieving, digital info-media world, most 21st-century Americans live in a flow of perpetual momentum with no end in sight. Neither extreme is good, so to balance ourselves we must consciously and continually self-regulate and impose as a rejuvenating or preventive measure the act of stopping all activity from time to time. Yes I said Stop. All. Activity.

I think pretty much all the time, about practical and bigger-picture things, reflecting on the state of the world, my life, my work—analyzing, understanding, observing and being as aware as possible every waking moment, and of course I am not immune to the stresses that everyday life and being human entail. This past weekend I slept for almost an entire day. Not due of lack of zzzz's or being sick, depressed or eating bad food, but simply because after everything I've been dealing with the past month or two, my mind, emotions and body needed me to temporarily shut down. I had nothing pressing going on, which the wisdom in my body knew and said to me, as it does every now and then, *Time for a rest.*

Just like bears that hibernate each winter, we need to take a periodic pause—especially after or during a busy, challenging or stressful period—to let our bodies be still on all levels so we can reconnect, regroup, and emerge refreshed and re-energized to our lives and the tasks at hand. That means (gasp!) disconnecting from technology and interaction with other people, if possible, so as not to expend any physical, mental or emotional juice.

You can sleep or not sleep, but there should be no distractions or even sound, if you can swing it. And no thinking, no reading, no writing. And no guilt. Just luxuriate in nothingness. Schedule and treat it as if it were a doctor's appointment or a trip to a resort spa—because it is that crucial to your physical and mental health. In other words, why not give your body and mind a break before they break down on you?

Our society promotes getting it all done all the time, which can take its toll when not interspersed with some serious downtime, which most folks allow themselves only when things have become so bad they are physically ill. Keep in mind that even though you might be getting enough sleep and eating right and you don't have the flu, when you're dealing with ongoing stress, you burn a different type of energy, which needs to be replenished with rest. And resting is different from relaxing ... but if you can't rest, then relaxing is better than nothing!

Because I'm pretty good at daily maintenance, I am generally healthy and balanced (including a weekly 24-hour no-computer-usage rule), so I know when it's time to heed the call in order to nip anything else in the bud. (And hey, most of the news, entertainment, activity, tweets, etc., you would be "missing" are nonessential, irrelevant, and often nonsensical anyway—so really, let it go!)

Stress is inevitable; it's how we manage it that counts, and rest plays a big part. Need help putting on the brakes? Block out those external forces so you can stop in your tracks in order to get back on the right one!

Mommie Dearest

March 12, 2013

In that famous scene from the movie about Joan Crawford, the renowned actress declares in a rage to her daughter Christina, "*No wire hangers—ever!*"

Hopefully you did not grow up with that kind of extreme abusive relationship, but it is not so farfetched to think that as an adult you might be *treating yourself* like Cinderella's evil stepmother on steroids from time to time, subtly, overtly or subconsciously beating yourself up about even the most trivial or insignificant things. Until we recognize and do something about it, we are often our own harshest critics when we need to be our most compassionate caregivers.

Do you speak nicely and are you kind to yourself, especially in the tape that runs in your head? Do you take care of your body by eating healthy when you're hungry, dressing appropriately for the weather, getting enough sleep, nursing yourself when sick, exercising, resting and *playing* on a regular basis? Do you allow yourself to express any emotion you are feeling—anger, sadness, frustration, joy, laughter—in an appropriate and timely manner? (Meaning, don't walk around emotionally constipated!) And especially if you are a mother of young children, responsible for an aging parent, a teacher, a healing professional or assuming any role of "official" caregiver, are you taking care of yourself as much as you take care of others?

Or perhaps on some level you operate like a neglected "orphan," walking around searching outside yourself, doing anything for that feeling of warmth and nurturing (or a continuation of it if you did have it as a child). The bottom line is we can't rely on someone else—spouse, partner, boyfriend/girlfriend, parents— to provide this for us; as *mature* adults (which has nothing to do with age) we should strive to be emotionally, physically, financially and intellectually self-sufficient, and most important, loving toward ourselves.

Whether or not you had a positive experience with whoever raised you, learn to nurture yourself as if you were your own precious child. When we are able to "mother" ourselves, it becomes a lot easier to give and receive love and compassion with those closest to us, and even with strangers. It doesn't matter if you are ill, out of work, or frustrated with a relationship or the state of the world—if we each commit to healing ourselves and take responsibility for our own well-being, we will begin to see positive change around us in big and small ways.

And to all the men out there, gender doesn't matter—we each have a gentle feminine nature within us that we can call upon and develop, just as we also have a macho warrior spirit!

So tonight when you go to bed, tuck in that little girl or boy within you, maybe drink some tea, read a story, and tell yourself you are sublimely cherished and grateful for all that you are, because as Lenny Kravitz's Mama said,[9] "Your life is a gift" and "Love's all that matters."

CHALLENGING TIMES

Sending Out an SOS

September 21, 2010

At a recent and much overdue reflexology session with my friend Noga Kreiman, I tried to sum up the tumultuous happenings within and around me these past couple of weeks, resulting in my visit to her. As we looked out the window at the fallen trees in her Park Slope backyard, she very aptly said, "Sounds like you had your own personal tornado!"

Last week, violent weather unleashed its power on much of the Northeast, with the NYC area hit pretty hard. If you weren't addressing the external collateral damage or power outages it caused, there's a good chance you were dealing with some other sort of inner or outer turmoil in your life.

In times like these, it's important to embrace the destruction and changes taking place, recognizing that often old structures and behaviors need to be demolished and uprooted in order for new ones to be rebuilt stronger and better. Don't neglect whatever the eye of the storm and its aftermath are telling you to pay attention to.

We also need to ask for help when we need it, as difficult as it may be to admit, and take that step to reach out. Staying isolated is a fast track into a downward spiral, like a twister that touches down and needs only seconds to wreak arbitrary havoc.

So if you are a bit distressed, or feeling like Sting circa 1979, don't wait for a hundred billion bottles to wash up on the shore;[1] send out a message to someone who will be a lifeline and bring you safely back to drier land and calmer skies.

Thank the Turkeys Too!

November 23, 2010

Whenever the fourth Thursday in November rolls around, we are meant to reflect on all the blessings in our lives. Traditionally, that would imply appreciating all that is good or positive, everything that brings us joy and happiness, or the things we could not live without. While that is certainly warranted, why not also be grateful for the funky, not-so-positive, annoying and pain-in-the-you-know-where stuff—the people, things and situations that challenge us, push our buttons, or make us feel uncomfortable.

As the saying goes, "There are no problems, only opportunities." Our crises and difficulties are chances for us to test our mettle, see what we're made of, and become stronger and wiser for it. They are occasions for us to make course corrections, adjust, fine-tune and put ourselves back in balance or on track—or perhaps on a different, better track. If life went smoothly all the time, we wouldn't have to dig deep, really look at ourselves, search within for answers, or find new, creative ways of doing things. Innovation is problem-solving at its most basic level (just watch those Dyson commercials), so where would we be without all the problems we've had?

Whether you're unemployed, having a health crisis, or having trouble in your personal or professional relationships, take a step back and see what the Universe is trying to show/teach you. Remember, those carbon atoms wouldn't become diamonds without extreme high pressure and heat.

When looking back on this year, figure out what now needs to be basted and tasted and what fat should be trimmed. Be thankful not only for the bird you are about to eat (or Tofurky if that's more your style), but for all those "turkeys" in your life—the folks and circumstances that gave you stress and grief but also compelled you to overcome those obstacles and become the person you are today.
Happy Thanksgiving!

You Are Not Alone

December 14, 2010

As a career/life coach, I have a unique vantage point to observe all types of people and notice certain trends and patterns that emerge. In addition to my clients, there is my circle of friends and family as well as my own experience, since I too am not immune to it all!

Lately the theme has been that of the warrior being challenged in at least one aspect of life, confronting unpleasant people or situations, dealing with loss, or relentlessly fighting a seemingly uphill battle at every turn. If you've been feeling tested (or testy) in the areas of relationships (all kinds), work (too much or not enough of it) or finances ('nough said), or are having a health or identity crisis—essentially, the stuff of life—raise your hand and know that you are not the only one who's been beaten up these past couple of months.

As difficult as it may be, the key is to acknowledge and recognize through all the discomfort/frustration/stress where growth has occurred, understanding has transpired, and wisdom will eventually come. Don't spend too much time figuring out *why* things have been going the way they have—instead, save your energy for *what can I do and learn as a result of what I've been through and how can I incorporate these newfound strengths moving forward?*

"Misery loves company" is a phrase we've all heard. It's not a concept that I would normally promote, but in these times of technological isolation and social media's "look at my fabulous life" updates and photos, there is comfort in knowing we're not the only ones struggling and it's OK to share the truth of how we're *really* doing.

The trick is *not* to have a pity party but to find community and provide mutual support; to take a collective heavy sigh and deep breath and have a good laugh about it, knowing that we're all in a similar boat, and do what we can to make things better. At end of the day we are all human, and we can offer one another a hug and a smile to get us through the hard times, which are always temporary.

Sorting out the who, what, where, when, why and how of what's been going on can be helpful too, and it requires digging a little deeper to see the lesson in the lickin' and the light at the end of the tunnel.

Out of Control

January 11, 2011

Some days you wake up and your computer decides not to work. A snowstorm hits and your flight is canceled or the sanitation department neglects to plow your street. Your Internet connection goes down for three days ... There are millions of things each day that are completely out of our control.

A good way to handle situations like these is to know that something positive will come as a result. The saying "there are no problems, only opportunities" is a good mantra to lean on. Being snowed in allows you to catch up on sleep, spend more time alone and/or with family, and clean the apartment. Having to live unplugged and actually pick up the phone can be refreshing, and having the hard drive replaced may solve other mysterious problems the computer was having!

Our goal is to use our time and energy in ways that suit us best when we have the freedom and choice to do so. And when we don't have that option, it's about making the best of it—because we *can* control our reactions, thoughts, words and deeds in whatever situation we find ourselves, whether or not it's to our liking. Unfortunately, when people are unable to control them, other influences can easily penetrate, and in a worst-case scenario can lead to devastating effects like what we saw recently in Tucson, the lessons of which we have yet to fully understand.

Over the holidays I read a book about Nelson Mandela, who spent 27 years in prison and whose tiny cell I saw with my own eyes when I visited Robben Island. Talk about having a controlled and measured response! Being incarcerated as a famous political leader, he could not change his circumstances, but he could decide how he maneuvered within them. By doing so, he sharpened his character, perceptions and strategy so that when he was freed and went on to govern and unite the country, he was more than prepared—and he did it in a spirit of reconciliation and forgiveness to boot!

One way to take control of your life is by asking for help. Because people live in their heads so much, having an unbiased, supportive person to talk to can give you a fresh perspective and new ideas, so that you can respond more effectively to whatever is happening around you. And that signals to the Universe that you are ready to make changes for the better, so it can too do its part! Then before you know it you'll be in Control² once again and rocking out like Janet Jackson did back in the day.

The Heat Is On /
Under Pressure

August 2, 2011

When we long for life without difficulties, remind us that oaks grow strong in contrary winds and diamonds are made under pressure. —Peter Marshall

My Personal Growth Gabs, which for well over a year have been sent out weekly, have been a bit erratic lately. I have been juggling several balls and doing the best I can in the time I have, with the resources at my disposal, and frankly, for the most part, have been kickin' some butt managing it all.

Although I have not received any direct monetary compensation for these PGGs, I *have* received an overwhelmingly positive response, which provides a level of satisfaction, joy and a sense of obligation for me to consistently give you some food for thought, inspiration and perhaps a chuckle to start your week.

But sometimes life gets to be too much all at the same time, and as another PGG says, **Something's Gotta Give**. The good news is that these times are always temporary.

When I was in Tunisia during Ramadan a few years ago, our guide could not eat or drink the entire day while he was educating us about the history and architecture of his country and taking care of all our needs. When I expressed my concern for his working under such conditions, he replied in the calmest, most Zen way, which only a person who is fasting while working 10-12 hours a day in the heat could say, "There are no problems, only opportunities."

Between the extreme summer temperatures, the public pressure felt from the debt ceiling, and other world problems, the many decisions and twists of fate that have been thrown my way—all while trying to throw a celebration for the last 10 years of my life—were an exercise in self-worth, focus and discipline. Let's just say a few of my carbon atoms have definitely transformed into diamonds, or at least crystallized!

I've chosen a journey that includes many challenging situations, having to prove myself and my tenacity, putting everything I preach into practice, and being able to turn on a dime, process things quickly, and ask for help. I've been getting quite the workout, that's for sure, and have felt like a ninja warrior most recently, but am so grateful because I am stronger and better for having gone through it all.

Feeling a little Under Pressure[3] yourself? Don't be afraid to walk through the fire and become a lean, mean diamond-making machine. At some point, you'll figure out what the heck and why, and what the benefit of all that was, understanding that everything happens in time and on time, to keep going and growing to become the mighty oak that you are!

The Roof Is On Fire

August 16, 2011

In 2009, southern Australia experienced some of the worst bushfires in over 20 years. But the climate and landscape make them a regular occurrence, and many flora and fauna have adapted over time to use these periodic blazes to fertilize their soil, spread their seeds, and regenerate more quickly. New species that can thrive in such conditions have been introduced, and folks in many places have even used controlled forest fires to remove underbrush and clear land for other constructive uses.

So with all the heartache and devastation that accompanies such incidents, it's important to remember that there is a positive and negative aspect to everything, and even disasters can ultimately be productive and have a silver lining. One thing is for sure: You cannot ignore a fire.

Sometimes we get to the place where destruction is required so a situation can be addressed/corrected/acknowledged and/or given the opportunity for something new and improved to exist. The riots in London, the stock market and debt ceiling madness, the crises in Syria and Somalia, extreme weather, and other "fires" here and around the world are ablaze, calling us to pay attention to them in one way or another. It's up to us to know what needs to be hosed down and what simply needs to burn, baby, burn.

In many ancient cultures, it is said the mythical phoenix dies many deaths by bursting into flames, only to return, rising from its ashes for all eternity. As you look upon the landscape of your life, what needs to be consumed or let go of in its current form in order to be reborn more magnificently?

Can't quite see through the smoke or feel the heat? You may need some outside perspective to show you which fires need to be put out, which need to be stoked, and where you might need to have one lit under your butt so that something better can sprout up in its place, allowing you to move forward in any area of your life. Look around to find the right accomplice that will either be the spark to Light Your Fire[4] or help you with Burning Down the House[5] ...

Fear Factor

August 30, 2011

The only thing we have to fear is fear itself. —FDR

Do the thing you fear the most, and the death of fear is certain. —Mark Twain

It used to be that scary movies only came out around Halloween, and there were just a handful at that. Nowadays they seem to be released throughout the year in waves and are more creepy, disturbing and bloody than ever.

Besides the usual monster mashes and alien invasions, there are the stories that prey on our defenselessness to natural disasters, biological vulnerabilities and other such forces beyond our control. Then there are the films and TV shows that simply glamorize and cool-ify violence and revenge as well as people who are clearly negative, like serial killers, drug dealers, vampires, ghosts and witches. That last group scares me the most because it is slowly but surely desensitizing us to characters with qualities we should not want to be chummy or fall in love with. But I digress ...

When it comes to our "real" lives, there are all sorts of metaphoric and literal things that go bump in the night, but the biggest one—and the root cause of all the others—is the fear of the unknown. Whether wondering what that noise in the basement is; what havoc a major hurricane, earthquake or terrorist attack will wreak; where your next meal, paycheck or retirement income will come from; or what happens when you have to speak in front of a crowd or after you take your last breath ... all the possibilities that can run rampant in your head boil down to one outcome: not knowing what the outcome is.

Most humans, especially Americans, and particularly New Yorkers, like to control everything. And because we are constantly active and living in this 21st-century distraction-filled, overstimulated world, the paradox and irony of the antidote to the fear of the unknown is, for many, the biggest fear of all: knowing ourselves.

The best way to deal with any fear or anxiety (no, not grabbing a Xanax) is to be in the present and confront what is right now, not what was or what could be. And to be in the present, you have to be with yourself.

By being in touch and comfortable with who you are and what you know and are capable of, you can take control of your life in a healthy way and come to trust in the process of a Universe that is always conspiring for your good. At the same time you must be vigilant and discerning as to what might be posing an actual threat or leading you astray. The goal is to balance that faith and trust with information, knowledge and understanding by being practical, realistic and prepared without becoming or succumbing to an alarmist, getting caught up in others' fears, or letting your imagination run wild—because it's almost never as bad as we think it will be.

There is a school of thought that says the opposite of love is fear, which makes sense since the way to overcome fear is with courage, a word whose Latin root means "heart," the muscle we use to express—you got it—love. So whatever you are currently afraid of, Put a Little Love in Your Heart[6] and notice the fear starts to melt away.

Feeling like the Lion in the Land of Oz? Learning to discern when your fears are real or imagined will help you develop the courage to move forward on your own yellow brick road. You'll be stronger, braver and wiser for having made the leap of faith to a new normal where you will wonder, *What was I so afraid of in the first place?*

Joni Mitchell Never Lies

September 13, 2011

Don't it always seem to go, that you don't know what you've got 'til it's gone.[7] —Joni Mitchell (via Janet Jackson)

I recently read that we have about 100 billion neurons in our brains, which is nearly equivalent to the number of stars in the Milky Way, further illuminating my belief that "macrocosm and microcosm are mirrors of each other."

We are all experiencing some facet of the same reality, some piece of a greater whole (which is why so many of you wonder how I could know what's going on in your life every week ...!). Until we start to truly comprehend that concept, there can be no real progress and we kiss that bright, shiny future goodbye.

At some point in our lives we have all suffered or been witness to the loss of loved ones, a job, our health, money, minds, homes, pets, friends, freedom, security, dignity, identity and the list goes on. And it seems we've been losing more than ever over the past 10 years, doesn't it?

When so many experience loss at the same time, it provides an opportunity to bond and elicits an empathy that might not normally be there. The challenge is to keep this awareness on a daily basis so we can honor each other and appreciate what we have when we have it, but at the same time be sure we don't fall into a perpetual pity party or throw in the towel, because if we work at it and are patient enough and have the right perspective, Things Can Only Get Better.[8]

Loss also moves us to seek purpose and meaning and to recognize what is important in life, which is pretty much the same for everyone. The more of us who embrace that fact, the more we will desire and take responsibility for creating peace and understanding in our own worlds.

Looking for a little more Kumbaya[9] these days? Take some time to see that your glass is indeed half-full, notice the silver lining all around you, and channel my practical Pollyanna so you can have peace in your piece of the pie, and make the best of what you've got, way before it's gone.

Beauty in the Breakdown

April 24, 2012

When we are no longer able to change a situation ... we are challenged to change ourselves. –Viktor Frankl

I recently read about a pill being developed that would erase unpleasant memories, kind of *Eternal Sunshine of the Spotless Mind*-ish. Of course I was appalled. It's bad enough the American public is seduced by quick fixes to deal with many physical ailments that a simple change in diet and exercise, a reduction in stress, a healthy does of self-love, or a little mind/body/spirit elbow grease would take care of. Now they want to get rid of negative memories?!?! We're already a society that overeats, overdrinks/drugs, over-sexes, over-technologizes, overworks and over-reality-shows to avoid what we're feeling!

There's a saying that many athletic coaches and trainers use: No pain, no gain. Yes, that can certainly apply to losing 20 pounds or training for a marathon, but it also applies to our inner workouts. As humans we like to avoid pain as much as possible, but pain can be a very useful tool if we let it. Emotional, mental, physical or spiritual/soul pain shows us where we're out of whack, where attention needs to be paid, and where adjustments must be made in order to learn and grow in any area of our lives.

To the extent that you are "asleep," the Universe is going to use some big ol' version of its alarm clock to wake you up and give you a big kick in the butt to do something about it. And a kick in the butt doesn't feel too good, but we all need one now and then to propel us into action. Most of us don't want to endure prolonged suffering, so the pain forces us to take action. In other words, as I mentioned in an article I was featured in on WellandGood.com, we often need to have a breakdown in order to have a breakthrough.

Remember that without pain we wouldn't know joy. When we are experiencing something akin to the "dark night of the soul," think of the caterpillar that thought the world was over just before it became a butterfly and that "it's always darkest before the dawn." Sometimes we just need to go there; these are the times that are meant to test our mettle and force us to rise up like the phoenix from the ashes in order to evolve into a better version of ourselves—and who wouldn't want that?

So if you feel you're about to crack, you've been sleepwalking a little too long, or you need someone to push you off that diving board, just Let Go,[10] jump in— what are you waiting for? It's time to discover the amazing beauty in whatever type of breakdown is occurring in your life.

You, Me & Dupree

May 14, 2014

If you are like me, my clients, family, friends and the rest of the world, you've been through some *stuff* the past six months (well more like the past two years ... oh heck, since the Fall of 2008!) that has tested, stretched, stressed and made you confront some not-so-pleasant realities about yourself, your life, and the people in it.

This meant lots of changes, whether forced upon you from the outside—i.e., having no choice but to move; getting laid off from your job; dealing with a divorce, breakup, or loss of a loved one—or internally, i.e., you were so sick of yourself or your situation that you had to do *something*, not the least of which was to change your perspective or finally accept the reality of how things are, rather than how you imagined or wished them to be.

The more challenges you have and the more you resist, the worse things get. This has been a time of "go with the flow," so whatever you've been through, know that it is exactly what you needed to make you stronger and get you to where you need to be next.

A lot of my work is about teaching you to trust yourself, have faith in the process, and possess the patience to let life unfold as it should—even with those bumps in the road and unexpected twists and turns along the way. As long as you are intimate, honest and honoring with and of yourself while consistently being in action (which is sometimes inaction), whether internal or external, have confidence that things will shake out the way they are supposed to, in time and on time, in whatever form the Universe deems is best for you.

It all starts with knowing and owning who you are, where you're at, what you truly want, and realizing you have the power to be the fullest, deepest expression of yourself if only you make it your responsibility and yours alone. It means we have to grow up!

One of the tools I gave those ninth-graders last month (see **Life Class**)—which I refer to as a superpower—was to be grateful whenever things get a little rough. Like those magic words "Open Sesame!," by simply focusing on something you can be thankful for, all of a sudden the pressure is lifted and a metaphorical door or window opens to let in a cool breeze, provide an answer to that riddle, or reveal a hidden treasure.

So no matter what you've been through recently, make sure you see the gift in the gristle, which is GROWTH. Give it up with a great big letting go of the past, and exhale heartfelt gratitude for whatever life handed to you, having gotten through it, and embrace all the good you've gained and have yet to experience as a result.

Once the dust settles, why not take a little time to survey the lay of the land so you can sort out who's who and what's what? Because when you do, you'll realize you should probably thank that unexpected messy house guest who disrupted your home, but in the end left it better off than it was when he got there.

Attitude of Gratitude

July 8, 2014

When author and self-help/relationship guru Iyanla Vanzant was asked what her prayer is, she answered that she had three. The first one is "Help!" The second is "Help now!" And the third is "Thank you."

Yesterday I went to return a bunch of DVDs to the library and there was a ridiculously long, slow-moving line. At the end of a hot and humid workday, when all you want to do is get home and sit in front of the fan or AC, the patience of many was being tested. But rather than succumbing to the apparent frustration of the situation, I instead turned to my practice of gratitude to keep me calm, cool and collected. "Thank goodness the library even exists," I thought to my-self. "Thank goodness for all the free movies I've watched—many I hadn't even heard of but because they do not cost me anything I took a chance and discovered a variety of films that I have thoroughly enjoyed and been inspired by." Suddenly the waiting was not such a big deal after all.

As the temperature starts rising, and NYC tempers start rising with it, it's good to keep that superpower (as I de-scribed it to my ninth-graders; see **Life Class**) in your back pocket to use throughout the day and cultivate an attitude of gratitude as part of your overall MO. Many studies and notable folks have promoted the benefits and magic that the energy of gratitude unleashes; whether writing a daily list, speaking it to others in your life, or silently acknowledging all the things you are thankful for as they arise in and around you, gratitude opens your heart and is the best way to celebrate your life, stay grounded, and reduce your stress no matter what.

Yes, we all know that Oprah keeps a gratitude journal, but even tough-guy media mogul and bison king Ted Turner, in some of his darkest hours in the midst of a huge corporate mess and painful divorce, said that's what kept him going. Every night before he went to sleep he would think about everything in life he was grateful for, and that helped get him through to another day.

Of course it's easy to be grateful when things are going your way, you got lucky, or your prayers were answered, but what about in the midst of a difficult situation or for the things we take for granted and hardly even notice anymore?

It's not always easy when you're in the moment, but just try breaking out some appreciation when dealing with serious challenges and/or their aftermath (i.e., taking care of a sick/aging parent, being laid off from your job, breaking up with a longtime partner, facing a debilitating illness or physical disaster), and focus on whatever good the situation is allowing you to experience right then and there. Remember to think about other hard times you've gone through in the past—in hindsight you were always glad they happened, right?

There are so many ways and moments that we can use gratitude, not the least of which is in our everyday interactions—whether with friends, family, foe or stranger, the common courtesies of "please" and "thank you" go a long way and are indeed deposits in the gratitude account.

And the little things and everyday surroundings we take for granted are not to be overlooked; this truly is the stuff of life: "Thank you for the roof over my head, my functioning brain, my ability to dance and listen to music, all the work I've done on myself to get to this point. For the fresh air, sunshine and easy access to the ocean as well as the mountains; the rain that makes the leaves green and the air that those leaves create so I can breathe. For the good friends and people who support me and make me laugh ..." You get the idea.

It's even become automatic now that when I sit down to eat a meal, I briefly pause to silently give thanks for the fact that I have food before me and appreciate the nourishment it gives; the miracle of Nature; the variety of options available to me; all the hard work it took to get it here; the people at the farmer's market and grocery store; the fact that I had the money buy it and my ability to cook, see, smell, taste and digest it; and the pleasure it gives me. It takes only a few seconds to encompass that recognition and all those thoughts into one acknowledging feeling, because when you really think about it, it truly is a blessing. (P.S. I LOVE food.)

And, as I approach completing my seventh year as a professional coach, I am beyond grateful to all my clients, who trust me with their time, energy, journey and dollars, and allow me the opportunity to do something I truly love that helps others to grow and heal their lives—which in turn has helped me to grow and heal mine. And for the readers of my PGGs who allow me to express myself in a creative way that many find beneficial and entertaining: *Thank you! Thank you! Thank you!*

It's true, as Nietzsche wrote and many songs attest, that "what doesn't kill you makes you stronger,"[11] so if you can't quite see the silver lining in the clouds around you, pause for a few moments to take a closer look and soon you'll be able to taste the rainbow of *your* life.

SELF-REFLECTION

The Passion of Passover

March 30, 2010

New Testament or Old, Facebook fan of Moses or Jesus, you
don't have to be a religious person to extract some nuggets
of truth from any of them. As someone who founded an
organization with the tagline "Recognizing Our Unity;
Celebrating Our Diversity," I'm always trying to see the things
we share in common that are in places we often think
are so different, especially if you look through the right lens
with the right attitude.

This time of year we are reminded of some good old-fashioned
foundations of personal growth—trust (in oneself, others and in
something bigger than oneself), faith, perseverance, forgiveness,
liberation, rebirth. Without their official branding, the Ten
Commandments and Golden Rule can offer you some guidelines
for a happy and fulfilling life, if you just think of them as good
advice from a friend or coach. Or even a TV commercial.

Be open to wisdom and inspiration no matter what form they
take, and like wearing those 3-D glasses at the movie theater,
learn to view things from many perspectives.

This is one of my personal specialties; I can look at the same
thing that you do and see something completely different, turn
it upside down, or see how it might be more or less significant
than you think it is. Taking a step back and trying to connect all
the dots between things that might seem totally unrelated will
help you understand whatever epic journey you're on ...

Slow Down, You Move Too Fast

June 1, 2010

The unofficial start of summer is traditionally accompanied by a more relaxed, go-with-the-flow attitude. Years ago, re-runs were shown on a very limited number of TV channels, and there was no Internet to entice/distract/constrain us from being outside enjoying the warmer weather and longer days.

With our 21st-century, 24/7 lifestyle, this means that we must consciously take time to disconnect from technology and reconnect with Nature and ourselves.

Like that cool special effect in big blockbuster movies, we need to pause midair and get a full 360-degree view of what is going on around us so we can take the precise action to defend and/or advance who we are and what we want.

Whether in the park or at the beach, be sure to take a moment to reflect on where you really want to be going and why, rather than just moving unconsciously from one activity to the next, day after day. If you've been feeling anxious or not in control, take that figurative or actual remote out of your hand, put it on slo-mo (or even pause), and I guarantee you'll be Feelin' Groovy[1] in no time!

Preparing for Liftoff

June 15, 2010

Over the weekend I attended a double feature of documentaries at the Explorers Club and was particularly moved by the film *Man on a Mission*, which follows the lifelong journey of multimillionaire video game celebrity/genius Richard Garriott and his dream to become the first second-generation American astronaut.

Now, I'm not a "space cadet" (as I learned such enthusiasts are called), but I did become enraptured by this extraordinary man's quest, despite several obstacles, millions of dollars, and intense physical and mental training to manifest his desire to follow in his father's footsteps. Like any other person with an eye on the prize, he just did whatever he needed to make things happen, and it's a truly inspiring real-life, albeit supersized, tale.

But besides making groundbreaking history and removing barriers to space travel, Garriott described his experience as transformational—as many who return from orbit do— because of what's called the "overview effect," seeing Earth from outer space and the internal shift and revelations that transpire as a result.

Yet you don't have to endure zero gravity or eat freeze-dried goop to gain a similar perspective if you just take a step back from time to time and simply *imagine* what your life would look like if observed from the International Space Station, and how it fits into the rest of this Big Blue Marble we inhabit. Try reflecting a little moonlight on yourself and let that be the launchpad to a life that any Earthling or extraterrestrial would envy!

Summatime

June 22, 2010

One of my favorite songs this (or any!) time of year is Will Smith/DJ Jazzy Jeff's "Summertime."[2] Nearly two decades old, it still has a timeless, classic vibe and sweet groove that embodies the flava of the season.

With the solstice now behind us, summer has officially started. We're in the midst of many endings and beginnings—school finishes, camp commences; textbooks begone, trashy novels devoured; serious films scaled back, popcorn/vampire/explosion movies released in full force; beach and barbecue gatherings abound. For a couple of months, we allow ourselves to take more time than usual to enjoy outdoor, fun, social and recreational activities without much of the guilt or low priority often assigned to them the rest of the year.

We're also halfway through the year—a good time to check in with yourself to see if you need to rev up your engines, shift gears, or just cruise along with your roof down, taking in the scenery while listening to some fly tunes.

For many, you can simply let all the hard work you put in the first six months of the year marinate a bit more before putting it on the grill. But if you're far away from where you set out to be in January, feeling restless instead of relaxed, or not even sure what your focus should be with these long, hot days ahead, concentrate on making the most of your energy and time ... and then you can just sit back and unwind.

Into the Woods

July 13, 2010

There's a saying that warns about not seeing the forest for the trees, a metaphor for when one is too mired in details to recognize the big picture of whatever a particular situation encompasses, or your life in general.

These days, it is easier to get lost in the trees in the most unconscious ways. Now more than ever we are sucked into dealing with all the daily minutiae of responding to emails and texts, updating and reading tweets and Facebook posts, paying bills, cleaning out/up our homes/offices, etc.—all of which are, to a certain extent, necessary and make us *feel* productive, but they are not moving us forward or closer to our goals.

Fairy tales often center on the woods and the mysteries they appear to contain or reveal. Be sure to make regular visits—not just once upon a time—to a forest near you (and bring your journal!) to experience its magic and wisdom. But keep in mind that in those fairy tales, the "enchantments" that accompany the journeys always point to the fact that the answers, tools and courage our heroes seek already exist inside them, and as a result transformation occurs.

So the irony of that famous saying is that being *literally* surrounded by trees is one of the best places to be in order to see the forest!

But if you can't make it upstate or to the woodsiest part of Central Park for a few hours, imagine being carried by one of those Ents from *The Lord of the Rings* to take in a bird's-eye view of your situation, then let it guide you to living happily ever after!

Holiday Road

August 17, 2010

In case you haven't noticed, it's one of those times of year when New York City is overrun by tourists, many of them Europeans who take much of August for their "holiday." They generally have a minimum of four weeks off, and that often includes touring abroad. Americans can take a hint from that mandated break, and the old-world lifestyle of working to live instead of living to work.

Travel is an amazing vehicle for self-discovery and cross-cultural understanding, but you don't have to rely on a *Lonely Planet* guide or go on a fact-finding mission to Italy, India or Bali for a year to get to know yourself and how to really live. If you took time to reflect and rejuvenate on a more regular basis, things wouldn't reach a breaking point that might cause you to do something so drastic or exotic.

And you don't have to break the bank either. Vacation simply means to "vacate" from your everyday life—no matter what that means for you to recharge and acquire a different mindset. A simple change of scenery for even a day can do a world of good to give you fresh perspective on where you're at—especially now, before the new "school year" begins and you focus on the next set of goals.

As we approach these dog days of summer, it's a good time to check out in order to check in with yourself, whether you have a specific itinerary or you simply take a mental vacation from your daily routine. If you can't quite get it together or find the perfect destination, leave the comedy and calamity to Clark Griswold, and look for a smooth and easy getaway to your own personal version of Walley World!

Wherever You Go, There You Are

October 26, 2010

With Halloween approaching, we are bombarded with spooky images and haunted houses to remind us it's the time of year to face our deepest fears. But the majority of what frightens us isn't conjured from external sources. Like the creepiness that comes from being in a house of mirrors, what usually freaks people out the most is seeing themselves multiplied a hundred times!

When in our personal house of horrors, no matter how many cobwebs and shadows we encounter, know that we all have darker aspects of our personality and we're never confronted with anything we can't handle, so we should never be afraid. Whether our fears and ugly parts are real or imagined, the key is not to run from them. We need to shed light on the source of our anxieties and perceived inadequacies, get to their roots, and make adjustments that will bring us closer to the most fulfilled and peaceful versions of ourselves.

And like the end of a scary movie, it comes down to you and only you to fight for your life. There is no magic formula or genie in a bottle, no Calgon or knight in shining armor to take you away. Taking responsibility for your life centers you in who you are and what you want—fantasy and illusion, or simply ignoring things, move you further away. It's up to you to create your own happiness and what you want in your life, and to ask for help along the way.

So if you need to do a little exorcising of your inner ghouls and goblins, who ya gonna call?[3] Like the guys in *Ghostbusters* or those meddling kids in *Scooby-Doo*, you need to expose and expel the real causes of your heebie-jeebies and things that go bump in the night so you can make the changes you need to be all that you can be in the bright light of day!

Blast From the Past

November 30, 2010

One of my favorite artists from back in the day, Howard Jones, sang: "The old man said to me, said don't always take life so seriously. ... Try and enjoy the here and now, the future will take care of itself somehow."[4] And he happily cautions in the chorus, "Don't try to life your life in one day, don't go speed your time away."

Over the long weekend, I came into a newfound appreciation for the wisdom of his pop songs—beyond what the catchy tunes, cute face and big orange '80s mohawk hairdo did for me back then.

Fashion and music always come around again in slightly different forms. Nowadays, with this economy, everyone is cutting back and having to scale down and tap into whatever material and personal resources they have. It's a good time to reflect on what facets within you can be recycled and refurbished. What about yourself, someone else, or the situation can you look at and see with new eyes, appreciate and/or put to use in a totally different way? What blast from your past—whether a song, piece of clothing, relationship or talent—can you relish in now, but in a more profound way?

Not sure what gems you might have forgotten that can be dug up and polished for your greater good? Do some excavating to resurrect those parts of your life that have been dormant far too long, and by doing so, discover that indeed Things Can Only Get Better.[5]

Freeze-Frame

January 25, 2011

It's that time of year when the president of the United States delivers his annual address to Congress and the country, reflecting on the reality of where we are now and the direction he plans for us to go over the coming year and beyond. It's a snapshot of what's happening at this point in time and in our history; it is a laundry list of the tasks ahead and is meant to be both specific and visionary.

Since we're only 25 days into the new year, it's still a good time to think about what you want in the coming 340, so why not take these chilly days to snuggle up with a journal and write a personal state of the union for your life?

How are your unique gifts, talents and abilities uniting with your work? If they're not utilized in your current job, how do you express them in your everyday life? How are you connecting and uniting with the people around you, whether family, friends, co-workers or strangers? How is the internal vision of who you are and what you want uniting with the reality of your life at this moment? If you could freeze-frame your life right now and examine it 10 years from now, what would you think? What would you tweak? What concrete things do you want to achieve, and what is your overall vision for this year and beyond?

If you don't yet have all the answers, a great way to start is by using those questions as a guide, then explore, evaluate, organize and come up with a plan to lobby for and legislate all that you want to accomplish in your personal corner of the world. And when you're done, you can celebrate with a little dance to the J. Geils Band's catchy hit tune,[6] which you will then not be able to get out of your head.

Conjunction Junction

April 5, 2011

Synergy—the bonus that is achieved when things work together harmoniously. —Mark Twain

I find it curious that the words *desperate* and *disparate* sound so similar; although their meanings are distinct and technically have nothing to do with each other, I think there is a correlation.

A well-known strategy used by one group to influence power over another is "divide and conquer"; it keeps people, things, countries, ideas, religions and feelings separate and often opposed to one another. This way they are unable to come together as a unified force and don't have the strength to accomplish their goals and objectives, which disempowers them. It is an extremely effective tactic, regardless of whether the power desired or deserved outcome on either side is good or bad.

The most obvious place to observe this happening is in the military and political arenas, but there are more subtle ways that this truth can affect us in our everyday lives—within our families, at our jobs, in our neighborhoods, in the media and entertainment we consume, and often, within ourselves.

Lately I've noticed a lot of folks are feeling disjointed, fragmented and compartmentalized at best; discombobulated or defeated at worst. Everywhere we turn, there seems to be a sledgehammer creating wedges, with myriad distractions coming at us from all sides: It's us against them, head against heart, black vs. white, profit vs. purpose, logic battling intuition, young vs. old, material values vs. spiritual ones, mental vs. emotional health vs. physical health.

As the saying goes, we can't serve two masters—we must be unified in that which we revere and honor, integrate our *disparate* parts and connect to who we are, so that we can connect to others for the greater good. Because when we don't, we feel lost and alone, which can lead to feeling *desperate*. And that is never a good place to be—because decisions made out of fear and desperation are never the best choices.

So if you're having a little trouble synthesizing your yin with your yang, make sure you take some quality time for yourself; you need to arrange your internal and external parts so that just like Stevie and Paul's piano, they too can live side by side,[7] and you can live with yourself and others in perfect harmony.

The Blind Side

November 1, 2011

I walk. A lot. My feet are my main source of transportation, as my Manhattan abode and general goings-on allow me to do so with relative ease. It's nothing for me to walk 30 blocks instead of taking a subway, bus or cab. If the ride is going to be 25 minutes or less plus walking to/from the destination, I often prefer to hoof it for the fresh air, exercise and lack of crowds—I save a few bucks and sometimes it's actually faster! I put on my iPod, clear my mind, and de-stress with each step; I consider it a moving meditation and wonder what discoveries I'll make along the way.

But in the Big Apple with its hustle and bustle, we must walk with a little protective bubble around us to keep us sane and safe—because if we truly took in everything all at once there would be serious stimulation overload, and perhaps a few unpleasant experiences.

Sometimes though, people take being in their own world to the extreme. I regularly observe legally blind men and women fumble or wait at a corner, only to have folks of all kinds pass by them as if they were invisible. Perhaps a few notice but are not sure what to do or are uncomfortable approaching a stranger. I generally ask, "Do you need any assistance?" Sometimes the answer is "No thank you," but more often than not they just need to be pointed in the right direction, know if it's OK to cross the street, or confirm what block they are on. Other times I'm met with profound relief as they grab my arm while I escort them wherever they need to go.

It never takes more than a minute or two, and the fact that no one else seemed to care upsets me every time. All it means is being a little more aware of your surroundings, which is a good thing no matter what, while still maintaining your don't-mess-with-me NYC look and attitude as you strut your stuff.

But I realize there's also something deeper to be learned from these moments, especially when they occur more than once in the course of a week: What is it that I'm not seeing in my own life? Where is my blind spot? How can I do more to show others what they cannot see for themselves?

So big guy (or gal), asking for direction(s) is never easy, but we *all* need help now and then. Looking for some assistance getting from point A to B? Find someone, perhaps even me, to get you on the right path and walk you through, step by step, giving you as much or as little guidance as you'd like along the way!

Be Kind Rewind

November 15, 2011

We're working our jobs / Collect our pay / Believe we're gliding down the highway / When in fact we're slip slidin' away.[8] —Paul Simon

How is it that next week is Thanksgiving?! I'm not sure why the older we get the faster time seems to go, but coupled with the technological superhighway we've been on, the perception of it is certainly speeding up, and life is passing us by in the blink of an eye.

Between the boob tube, a gazillion distractions on the Internet, aimless nights out on the town, sales at the mall, and whatever the celebrity gossip channels and news media outlets are forcing us to focus on at the moment, it's easy to lose track of what we can control and create for ourselves.

And no matter what you do for a living, it's easy to let the daily grind eat up your days; it's even worse if you're not connected to your work in a meaningful way, and if you have others to care for on top of your own stuff, that adds even more to your load. Whew!

This is why it's so important to stop every now and then—daily, weekly, monthly, quarterly, the more the better—to see what's really happening in your life, rather than perpetually going through the motions to get through the day.

I am constantly reminding my audiences and clients that your time and energy are your most precious resources, so with only seven weeks left in the year, take this opportunity to check in to see if you've been using yours the way you said you would back in January. Have you checked off all the things you wanted to accomplish before the clock strikes midnight on December 31? If not, there's still a reasonable amount of time to do something about a few of them, I'm sure.

It's also that time of year when we reflect upon all the blessings in our lives—and no matter how challenging things might be, we can always find something for which to give thanks.

Because unlike the shows on our DVRs, we cannot simply rewind our lives and recover lost time, but we *can* review what has transpired in order to learn from our experiences and move forward with a better understanding and clearer purpose of whatever is next on the horizon.

Not sure where the minutes, hours and days are going, unsure of what you did with the ones you had, or feeling like you don't have anything to put on your gratitude list this year? Spend some time doing an instant replay of the past 11 months, and think about what you'd put on your highlight reel or what you want to add to it before the year ends. Then like Alanis,[9] you should find plenty to be thankful for!

Heart & Soul

June 26, 2012

Two weeks ago my mom was on the operating table for almost five hours while an amazingly skilled surgeon replaced a valve, bypassed a main artery, and did some serious zapping in order for her heart to function properly. I am more than happy to report that she is well on her way to recovery, and I know she will be better than ever as a result of the ordeal.

Since finding out she would have to go through this, and realizing I would be the primary caregiver especially for those first two weeks, I knew that there were several things I would learn, reaffirm, understand, and most important, practice as we embarked upon this journey ... so lord knows these PGGs will be chock full of my "takeaways" this summer!

Let's start with first things first: witnessing the simple yet miraculous fact that the body is built to heal. Our natural state is one of health, healing and wholeness, and we are always trying to get back to that place, even with little or no conscious effort on our part. When given enough time, the body will adjust so it can live—like the main artery the docs said had been so clogged and calcified that it must have happened over many years, because my mom's body had just naturally created its own way to get blood where it needed to go, and also how quickly she was functioning less than 24 hours after the extensive operation she endured.

I'm a *huge* proponent of alternative medicine and holistic/mind/body wellness, and I believe that most illness can be prevented and/or cured by diet, exercise, sleep, positive thoughts, understanding and healing the emotional roots of the disease, etc. ... But when it comes to fixing broken stuff, there is nothing like modern Western medicine for surgery—and it's pretty amazing what we can do these days.

Unfortunately I've had the opportunity to visit and know intimately many hospitals over the years. My mom was in a place known for its superior cardiac care, but what struck me about this particular hospital is that besides its excellent doctors, nurses and technical/medical reputation, the atmosphere of healing permeates the premises and radiates through just about everyone we interacted with.

It's a Catholic hospital, and I had never been in one of those before, so I wondered if perhaps that has something to do with it. There is a genuine feeling that the staff is there for patients as whole people, not numbers or cases, and almost as important, for keeping the family and friends of those patients as relaxed and stress-free as possible. In other words, I felt equally as cared for as my mother. (I knew we had chosen a great place when I noticed signs everywhere that say, "Please be quiet ... healing in process") They totally acknowledge that the caregivers are very much part of the patients' experience and are integral to their healing as well.

As a career/life coach and speaker on employee engagement, I am always talking about how aligning your work with your life creates the most fulfillment for you and also serves others. I was impressed with how the doctors and nurses seemed to share a common purpose, a deeper meaning to what they do and why they are there—and my guess is that it comes not only from "management" but from an inner connection to their work. And man, does it show!

Of course this is heightened by the fact that many have jobs that are quite often literally dealing with matters of life and death, and I'm sure they have their bad days and issues with co-workers, but nothing is perfect, and we should all strive to have workplaces as cohesive as that, regardless of the industry or business.

As I say in all my talks, we are living in extraordinary times; change and upheaval abound, causing us to confront the dis-ease in our lives. Wondering how you can create an atmosphere of healing and purpose wherever you need it? You may need to perform a version of open-heart surgery on yourself ... minus the anesthesia or rehab, and with an extra dose of Heart and Soul![10]

Validation Nation

July 24, 2012

The greatest gift you can give to the world is a healed life.
—Dr. Christiane Northrup

What is to give light must endure burning. —Viktor Frankl
(via Anton Wildgans)

Last month a white buffalo was born in Goshen, Connecticut, and its naming ceremony is taking place this week. This is a sacred and rare event in the Native American tradition, the significance of which varies in interpretation, but it's auspicious nonetheless, and at the very least is yet another sign of the extraordinary times in which we live.

We're at a point where we can no longer ignore the problems that on some level we've known all along we must address—whether climate change; the economy and our government; our physical, mental or emotional health; our relationships with ourselves, our family and our friends; or the gap between the fantasy of how we perceive our lives versus the reality of what they truly are. We must bring to light what is holding us back, stop living in denial or distraction, and take responsibility for our own happiness.

For many of us, our limitations are rooted in the infinite search for approval and the pain we feel when we don't get it, especially from those closest to us. Our culture seems to have exploited this, whether someone is singing in front of millions of people, walking on a red carpet, living in a literal or metaphoric glass house, or deemed worthy of receiving a rose from a bachelor or bachelorette—or more perversely, and often magnified by mental illness, strapping on a bomb in a crowded area, becoming a despotic ruler, or embodying a pseudo-character in a movie and committing mass murder, knowing the attention and infamy such an action will bring.

In this Time of the Season,[11] who's your daddy? Are you seeking approval from parents, friends, partners, bosses, the opposite sex, the same sex, Facebook likes, Twitter followers or the public at large? As comedienne Margaret Cho reminds us, we have to be ones that we want. We cannot be defined by others so let's get honest, let's get real with ourselves. Because when we choose to avoid delving into the deepest parts of ourselves, we turn to indulging or overindulging in unhealthy relationships, food, TV, work, the Internet, gossip and bullying, drugs, sex, alcohol, video games, gambling, movies, and so many other things to numb us. Instead of masking whatever feelings may be lurking beneath the surface, we need to walk through the fire; there are no shortcuts. And remember, if you can't feel the bad, that means you can't feel the good either!

We are the only ones who can give meaning to our lives, and we are constantly reminded of just how brief that life can be. We must dig deep within our souls to find the stuff we are made of and the things we must release in order to move forward, to heal our lives. We need to discover and then liberate ourselves from who or what is owning us by making us feel validated. That process may be uncomfortable, and yes, even painful. But in allowing ourselves to go there, we can then leave there once and for all. Our country and the world are depending on it.

Need a little help Digging in the Dirt[12] to open up the places you got hurt? Find someone, maybe even me, to help you tear up those roots and replant the seeds of healthy self-esteem that bloom just for you. Should you by chance attract an admirer or two, that's simply a byproduct of bringing your own special brand of beauty to a world that so desperately needs it.

Drop It Like It's Hot

August 13, 2013

If you're anything like me, many of my clients, and millions of humans, you are often your own worst enemy and harshest critic. Perhaps you set imaginary limits and keep yourself from experiencing all that life has to offer, holding back for "rational" reasons or because of subconscious thoughts based on irrational fears and silly untruths.

Since I can't clone myself (yet!?), I too sometimes need an outside brain to get a little perspective and see things I can't quite perceive within myself. And because the majority of my work as a coach involves listening, sometimes I, like all humans, just need to talk and be heard.

Therefore, I am ever-grateful for my closest friends and unofficial therapists who support me in various ways and set me straight (whether they know it or not!) with additional insights and tools I need to become unblocked, make adjustments, and move forward.

Because I spend an extraordinary amount of quality time with myself and practice what I preach/write, one thing I most definitely am is self-aware. So when I get to a point where I gain even more awareness of things I probably should have been aware of in the first place, I can fall into a cycle of beating myself up for not being aware *enough*! As my holistic healer friend Noga says, "Ah, the problems of being a conscious person!"

Along with a new awareness I recently gained came feelings of ickiness, shame, stupidity and all-around disgust for allowing things not to have clicked for me in a certain way until this point. This did not feel good, but in a twisted way it felt right because I was punishing myself, which seemed appropriate for the transgression against yours truly. Oh, how the ego loves that!

As I always say, your time and energy are your most precious resources. And punishing yourself or beating yourself up is a waste of those valuable commodities and serves no purpose (except that it can greatly adversely affect your health)! So what do you do?

I normally have a few tools in my toolbox to process such a spell, but thanks to Noga, I was introduced to a new one: Pretend the feeling is like holding a pen in your hand, and just drop it. DONE. GONE. ARRIVEDERCI. Since I have developed quite the strong muscle for being in the present and monitoring my thoughts, I simply needed to transfer this skill to eliminating useless, unproductive and destructive emotions! And guess what? It works!

So for this PGG, I really just wanted to share that. Wherever you're at in da funky club of life, you can always use a little more self-awareness, someone to talk to (with x-ray vision and supersonic hearing), perhaps even me, who can offer you some insights and tools, or a little help developing your own "presence" muscle.

Happy
March 11, 2014

While making a purchase last week, I must have been sub-consciously but overtly enjoying Pharrell Williams's snappy tune, which was playing on the store's sound system. The cashier, a young gal probably not more than 21, asked me, "Why do all adults love this song?"

Ahhh, youth. First off, I needed to comprehend the fact that I was one of those "adults" she was referring to, which took me a minute because I think I'm 25 … . She continued, "Yeah, my mom and aunts and all their friends get into it whenever it comes on."

The uplifting, catchy anthem could not have been released at a better time, after one of the harshest winters on record and accompanying the spring forward of our clocks that signals the imminent arrival of brighter days and warmer weather.

But I think the real gift is its simplicity—its airy, carefree, innocent vibe and powerful lyrics. It cuts through all the heavy stuff we deal with and are responsible for and asks our inner child to dance a little inside and out. Because let's face it, we all need a break from the warmongering, negative TV shows/movies/video games, political bickering, and multitude of challenges modern life presents us "adults" on a daily basis—even if it's for only 3:52 minutes.

A friend of my mom's whom I've known over 25 years saw me recently, and with a very perplexed look and completely serious tone asked, "When are you going to start aging?"

I just chuckled. I suppose good genes and moisturizer play a part, but I really attribute it to my frame of mind and life-style—I have learned to take care of myself physically and spiritually, and have the tools and discipline to manage my stress (trust me, there is plenty!). I honor and process my emotions, think positive thoughts, and do my best to live in the present and go with the flow, listening to my deepest self and paying attention to the world around me. I operate from my heart (and gut), not my head, and I value quality over quantity in relationships.

I realize that I am on a journey, and as long as I'm learning and growing and being of service, I am doing something right. I am creative and know how to relax. I'm a practical idealist. I laugh often and cry just as much, if not more. I love. I am committed to being as authentic, balanced and centered as I can be, knowing I'm not "perfect" and that's OK; I take one day at a time and understand that every problem is an opportunity in disguise, as hard as that might seem in the moment. I am grateful. And lastly, I shake my booty to groovy tunes as much as possible. So yes, I choose to be Happy, because happiness is the truth—and one of the keys to youth.

Still trying to figure out what happiness is to you?[13] Take one step at a time, knowing that you'll be just fine, then clap along if you feel like that's what you wanna do and make it so can't nothin' bring you down! Yeah.

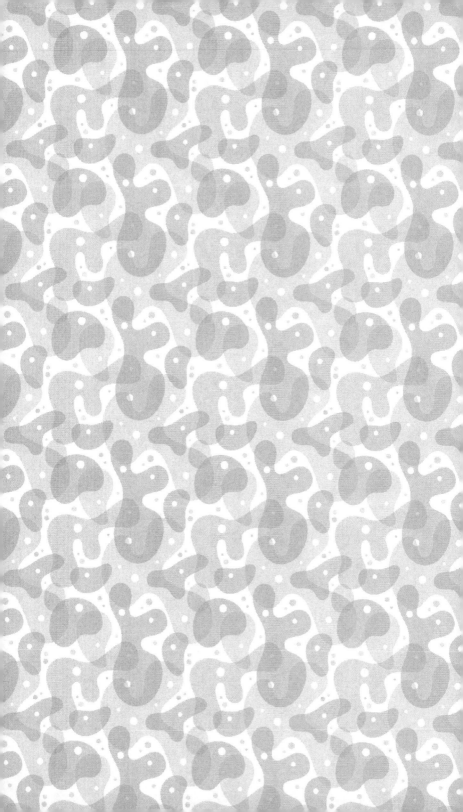

CHANGE & TRANSITION

Out With the Old, In With the New

November 2, 2010

Elections bring out the best and worst in people and politicians, especially in this contentious climate. But casting your vote in the broadest sense means that you are exercising your right to exist and participate in life.

I have a friend going through a major transition, trying to figure out what to do next, how to reconcile his past and secure his future; he has been doing a lot of soul-searching lately, excavating his talents, skills and passions. While he was in the process of shedding that old skin, I suggested he let go of his action-oriented descriptions, telling him, "You need to decide who you want *TO BE*, not what you want *TO DO*."

I am always recommending that folks spend time in and learn from Nature, because Nature just *IS*. When talking about patience and process, my favorite saying is, "The acorn does not become an oak tree overnight." Also remember that an acorn has the inherent DNA to become an oak tree—it doesn't question it. It just unfolds and grows as it should but will look and feel different at every stage of the process.

Many of my clients have recently had to confront being with people they had bad experiences with in the past or doing things they simply didn't like or enjoy two, 10 or 15 years ago. I let them know, however, that like those old clothes in the closet that you've outgrown or perhaps bought but never wore, or that simply don't suit you anymore—who you were then is not who you are now.

I have witnessed the transformations my clients have made. Because they have done the work, I know they will approach, interact with, and experience things in a vastly different way going forward, if only to show themselves that they have indeed changed.

So if you're not quite sure if you're an elm tree or an oak, or if you're thinking about doing something you've been fearful of in the past, maybe it's time to be like Christopher Lloyd's time machine and go *Back to the Future* to dig around, let go of certain things and adjust your outlook to make your present the very best it can be!

The Year of Living Uncomfortably

January 4, 2011

I recently read that "a person's success in life can usually be measured by the amount of uncomfortable conversations he or she is willing to have." Many people begin the year by starting a new exercise or other routine that can have them feeling sore or out of sorts, but doing this with your patterns of interaction and communication can also reap rewards. Like any muscle, growth happens outside of your comfort zone.

Maybe that uncomfortable conversation needs to be with your boss, that contact for your dream gig, your partner, a parent, your neighbor, that cute guy/girl you've been eyeing, or that celebrity you'd love to talk with, or maybe you just need to put yourself in a foreign social situation. But you also need to have that honest conversation with yourself in order to face the reality of your life as it is versus the way you'd like it to be—because the one common denominator in your life is YOU, and taking responsibility for why it is the way it is is paramount, if not always pleasant.

In other words, the good news is that by chatting with yourself on a regular basis, you can know what changes you need to make to move your life closer to your ideal!

Not quite feeling it? I say, "Fake it till you make it" and remind you that "insanity is doing the same thing over and over again and expecting a different result." So if things aren't going your way, why not try a slightly different approach from your usual MO? Or you can go whole hog and be like George Costanza in the *Seinfeld* episode where he does the exact opposite of what he would normally do, to some hilarious effects and success!

So this year, resolve to have those challenging conversations, not care what people think, try new things without worrying whether you'll look foolish, stand out in a crowd, and be OK with not being perfect. (Well, those were some of mine ... just insert whatever makes *you* uncomfortable.)

Wondering how to get from here to there? Like a personal trainer, motivate yourself to stretch those inner muscles, have that heart-to-heart with yourself, and make your discomfort as comfortable as possible along the way!

Changing of the Guard

February 1, 2011

Congress ushered in a new speaker of the House, Queen Elizabeth is thinking about abdicating so Prince William may actually have a shot at being king; Tunisia overthrew its longtime leader, and Egypt is on the brink of doing the same; American television staples Larry King, Regis Philbin and *ET*'s Mary Hart, whose careers took off around the same time Hosni Mubarak came into power, are all retiring. What is the world coming to?!

Change is certainly in the air, and tomorrow is the Lunar New Year, so it's another good time to start fresh for the next 12 months. What are you ferociously guarding in your life—and is it worthy of protecting, or are you just doing so because it's been that way for the past 30 years? What people, ideas, jobs, things or ways of thinking are you holding on to that are old, stagnant and outdated, have served their purpose, have overstayed their welcome, or just need to step down so that something better and fresher can take their place?

And what about that old persona you've been wearing? We're usually our own worst enemies, so maybe it's time to take a look at the dictator who rules our lives—benevolent or not—and see how we might be restricting ourselves or abusing our power; where we've fallen into a rut or how we might have outgrown our "schtick," perhaps needing a new audience to reflect back to us different facets of who we are.

Often things are so ingrained in us that we can't easily recognize them, and we need some deep reflection and outside perspective. After participating in a Visioning Workshop, then working with me for the next four months, a client has completely turned around her perspective, resurrected the true essence of who she is, embraced her new direction, and in turn literally looks like a different person—and 10 years younger!

Need a little help toppling your own outdated regime? Allow the repressed parts of yourself to rise up and have more say in governing your world, or at least get higher ratings.

Something's Gotta Give

March 15, 2011

As we watch with heartbreak and compassion the devastating aftermath of the earthquake in Japan, it's a good time to reflect on (or react to) where that tectonic plate is in your life that needs to be released of its tension. Where do you need to prevent a tsunami or nuclear fallout from occurring, or recover from one that just did?

We all have areas of life we tend to neglect more than others, allowing things to build up over time. Like Mother Nature's need to release her pent-up pressure through a variety of earth- and weather-based events, our unbalanced energy has to go somewhere. And when not addressed, it gets buried within us as fat or addictions, crushing debt, unhealthy relationships, dead-end jobs, physical or mental illness, or a general malaise until one day the walls come a tumblin' down—because if you don't take care of it, the Universe eventually will.

As the saying goes, we often need to have a breakdown before we can have a breakthrough; it's just life showing us where change is required. What emotions have been repressed that need to be released with a good cry or a sweaty workout? Is your mind about to crack (hopefully not the way Charlie Sheen's did, which on the surface appears entertaining but is no joking matter)? Is a relationship, career, job search or financial situation beyond repair or in need of a big ole tune-up? Is your body giving you a hard time?

Change is one thing that is certain in life, and it is most definitely in the air at the moment. Embracing it and going with the flow makes dealing with change easier and less stressful, so heed the wisdom from a certain '70s hit TV show, when Peter was going through puberty and the Brady kids sang, very groovily I might add, "When it's time to change, then it's time to change / Don't fight the tide, come along for the ride."[1] It means that "... you've got to rearrange who you are into what you're gonna be." (Try getting that song out of your head now ... Sha na na na na.)

Change is always good if we respond to it in the right way—by accepting our state of affairs and our responsibility in its creation, and by facing the fears of what actions are necessary to confront it, all the while knowing that we will be better, stronger and wiser for having done so. And we need to deal with the reality of the situation as it is, not as we would like it to be.

Not sure where the seismic activity or cresting river is in your life? Like Luke Skywalker or Jamiroquai, you can always Use the Force[2] to help you read the warning signs and find relief and/or recovery so you can avoid a full-on meltdown and instead enjoy the ride!

Don't Worry, Be Happy

June 7, 2011

In every life we have some trouble / But when you worry you make it double.[3] —Bobby McFerrin

As the saying goes, three things are certain in life: death, taxes and change. Change comes in all shapes and sizes, some scarier than others: climate change, career change, graduations, marriages, relationships, TV changes, sex changes, change of residences and regime change, to name a few—and June seems chock full of them!

The reality is that time keeps on slippin' into the future, so we have no choice in the matter of change, because like Kevin James' dancing in *Hitch*, "You can't stop this, you cannnoottt stop it ..."

Most folks have a hard time with change. We'd rather stay comfy and/or miserable than let go of our crutches and seeing what else life might have in store for us. We cannot control things, but we can control how we respond to them. We can resist and go kicking and screaming, or we can accept that change happens and just go with the flow.

Going with the flow means listening to yourself and giving yourself what you need at any particular moment. The best way to deal with change is to trust in yourself and be your own best counsel, so it's important to have that "muscle" in place as you navigate the whitewater rapids of feelings that come with this thing called life.

Change is not always fun, but it's almost always for the better because change forces growth, and growth is good. And once the change happens, we can't be like a goldfish that lived in a fishbowl its whole life and after it was put into the ocean continues to swim around in a little circle as if it were still in a bowl!

David Bowie tells us that time may change you, but you can't trace time.[4] So this summer, if you feel ready to be hatched, then fly, be free! Not quite like Mork's egg, more like Steve Miller's Eagle[5] or with the help of Bob Marley's Three Little Birds[6] and the wonder of that other Stevie who sings, "Don't you worry 'bout a thing"![7]

But if you're not quite ready to fly the coop, walk without those crutches, or swim in the big blue ocean, you may need to find somebody to Lean On[8] until you feel strong and can carry on ...

The Change-Up

August 9, 2011

When things aren't quite going your way, it's easy to fall into the grass-is-always-greener syndrome. But as the saying goes, before you judge a man (or covet his life), walk a mile in his shoes.

You don't have to turn back the clock, eat a magical fortune cookie, ride in a souped-up DeLorean, or relieve yourself in an enchanted fountain to discover that your life and relationships are exactly as they should be, or get the kick in the butt you need to make them better.

The fact is, our lives are the sum total of all the choices we've ever made until this point—a combination unique unto ourselves. That means we have, on some level, created the situation we've wanted or needed in order to learn and grow on this journey called life.

So whatever your state of affairs, take full responsibility for it. The good news is that if you don't like it, because you got yourself into it, you totally have the power to get out of it!

A lot of my clients right now are at the point of no return, where there's no more delaying the inevitable. The only thing they can do is go through—there is no way around, there is no way back—they need to make a change or take action in a certain direction because there's no alternative, whether because of forced external realities or an internal malaise and dissatisfaction that they can no longer withstand.

Why changes haven't been made up to now is a more complicated and varied topic for another time. Often it's a stronger sense of obligation to others, what *they* want or what would make them happy, that prevents us from moving forward to the beat of our own drum. But contrary to Hollywood movie plots, we are the ones who have to live in our bodies, so it's up to us to do what needs to be done. It's time to go big or go home.

Not fully convinced that you can move forward without going all topsy-turvy or time travel-y, or using some freaky fictional device to help you wake up and smell the coffee? Just take a moment to understand and appreciate where you're at and what changes you can make, so that you can experience whatever you need in order to be the best you can be, Right Here, Right Now.[9]

Let the Sun Shine In

May 22, 2012

There is a crack in everything / That's how the light gets in.[10]
—Leonard Cohen

I recently had my apartment painted, which is basically like moving without actually moving. The main reason I did it was to force myself to go through all of my belongings and see what should stay and what should go, clean all the nooks and crannies that never get looked at, and rearrange things in a better way. Well, it's working, but for various reasons it has been happening s-l-o-w-l-y ... and I just need to be OK with that.

In my PGG **The Present of Presence,** I mentioned that out of chaos comes clarity. And I'm always talking about process, how patience is a virtue and the consistent effort needed to make lasting change, **One Day at a Time**. I'm certainly getting some good practice right now!

It's been a great exercise to dismantle my external life, since most days I live and work on the internal side of things. Just as with physical surgery, sometimes you gotta literally open up, get in there, dig around, and rid yourself of and/or fix whatever is not working in order to begin healing and functioning more optimally. Like my client's ostrich with its head held high on her Vision Board, we have to deal with what is and take action, instead of keeping our heads buried in the sand expecting things to change.

With all the graduations and series, season and competition finales, as well as the loss of some famous folks, it's a reminder to say goodbye to life as a student, to an era, to characters and storylines, and perhaps to jobs, people, places and things, and especially to old personas we've outgrown. There are just times in our lives when we need to let it all go to make way for the new.

What needs to be opened up, dismantled and re-examined in your life? What is old and tattered and/or has served its purpose and should be released? What can be put back together in a new and improved way so you can more easily integrate ALL parts of yourself and more effortlessly move forward in the most positive way on this journey called Life?

Whatever area you feel stuck in, be sure to Ch-Check It Out[11]—because only when you look at things from a different perspective can you make different decisions. Having a hard time letting go of anything that's not Hot Stuff?[12] You may need someone, perhaps even me, to help you face the music and get you Stayin' Alive[13] in the best version of yourself now and beyond!

Reality Bites

January 7, 2014

Truth is a deep kindness that teaches us to be content in our everyday life and share with the people the same happiness. –Khalil Gibran

If you look for truth, you may find comfort in the end: if you look for comfort you will not get either comfort or truth—only soft soap and wishful thinking to begin with and, in the end, despair. –C.S. Lewis

New Year's always stirs up thoughts about what we want to change in our lives, but that means you need to have a good idea of what needs to change in the first place—and as the famous prayer says, have the serenity to accept the things you cannot change, the courage to change the things you can, and the wisdom to know the difference.

Getting to that accurate perception is the first step and might actually be more important than making the change; therefore perhaps our work this year is to "snap out of it" and instead see ourselves, situations and people as they really are, not how we'd like them to be. Then and only then can real change begin.

Humans, especially 21st-century versions, want what we want when we want it; our media and technology only make this worse, fueling our impulses and imagination with their magnified distortion of time, place and interaction; they enable us to delude ourselves more easily into thinking our situation is one way when it is in fact another; when we think a job, our health, or a relationship is positive when it's not, or vice versa. They distract us and make us forget that anything lasting is a process and requires massive amounts of reflection, patience and perseverance.

As the biblical saying goes, "Know the truth, and the truth shall set you free." It's not always fun getting there. Letting go of lifelong dreams and illusions as well as accepting ourselves, people and circumstances as they are—relinquishing any hope that they are or will become what or who you wish them to be—can be extremely painful and, in fact, feel like a death that you need to grieve.

The good news is that knowing and accepting the truth affords us a more profound, productive and meaningful life experience when we know what is real. When we live from that place, we can then make better decisions about addressing any situation, how to improve it or let it go— the more accurate the assessment, the more effective the solution can be.

Because of my talent for connecting the dots, cutting through the "crap," and getting to the root of things quickly and directly, my clients might not like what I have to tell them at first—yet they always come back to me days, weeks or years later and admit it was not necessarily what they wanted to hear but ultimately exactly what they needed at the time. (And saved them thousands of dollars in therapy!)

The truth can be overwhelming, but once you acknowledge it, you can really start to move forward. So before you seriously embark on any resolutions, begin there. It's strong medicine to start off the year, but it's essential if you want to get healthy in *any* area of your life.

Feeling certain that A Change Is Gonna Come,[14] but not sure how to make it happen? Find someone, perhaps even me, to be the doctor with the diagnosis *and* that Spoonful of Sugar[15] to help the medicine go down!

CURRENT EVENTS & GLOBAL PERSPECTIVE

Mercy Mercy Me

May 11, 2010

What's going on?[1] Whether socially or sensually, many have gotten it on[2] to Marvin Gaye's tunes, being enlightened and healed in a variety of ways as a result. You say you want a revolution? The Beatles told us it's gonna be all right.[3] And the Rolling Stones declared we can't always get what we want, but if we try sometimes, we get what we need.[4]

The turmoil taking place both here and across the pond (oil spill, flooding, volcanic ash clouds, tornadoes, bankrupt governments, elections up in the air, stock market plunges, foiled terrorist plot, political protests, strikes ... I could go on) can put you a little on edge if you really consider all these upheavals happening simultaneously. If you are feeling directly affected or anxious about them, there are ways to keep you in the groove.

Think about what crisis is bubbling up or spinning out of control in your own world—physically, emotionally or otherwise. Since we are all connected on one level or another, we can each create peace in our own piece of the pie. If we take responsibility to extinguish, learn from, and even prevent massive fires from burning up our individual lives, we'll be doing our part to keep things as collectively calm as possible.

So if you find yourself in stormy seas, stop and think about what might be stirring things up and how to get back on course. Because as Simon & Garfunkel suggest, finding that Bridge Over Troubled Water[5] will ease your mind ...

Déjà Vu All Over Again

March 22, 2011

I woke up Saturday morning and turned on the TV to find out that foreign military action had begun in Libya. What?!? I had missed the quickie UN resolution that took place Friday and watched live as the media scrambled, trying to decipher what was going on. And all the time I'm thinking, Is this really happening *again*?

A sinking feeling came over me. Yes, I was happy that Lindsay Lohan was out of the news, but to be replaced by coverage of another US multilateral intervention? Yikes! Spring has most certainly sprung.

One thing we know for sure is that history, unfortunately, often repeats itself. War is rarely simple or justified. We've had so many movies and video games laden with violence that as a society we've become desensitized. What we see on the big screen is now starting to unfold in reality on the small screen. There has been so much massive tragedy and destruction in the last several years, both natural and man-made, that it doesn't even faze us as much as it should. As long as we still have our *DWTS*, *American Idol* and *Jersey Shore*, we can numb ourselves and tune out. When will we ever learn?

Because we've been lulled into such a state of complacency and so many of us are dealing with financial survival, the gravity of what happened this weekend is barely registering our Richter scale. But if you can't comprehend and connect globally, then at least reflect and act locally.

There's an old song that says, "Let there be peace on Earth, and let it begin with me."[6] So the question is: Are you at war with yourself? Is your head battling your heart and gut about which direction it wants to go? Is your body struggling with your mind and not doing what you need it to do? Where in your life is history repeating itself? What conflicts are constantly being re-created with different uniforms, labels, situations and countries?

As Bob Marley sang, "We don't need no more trouble,"[7] not only with our multifront wars in the Middle East, but with our wars at home on the middle class, women's health, Muslims, and homosexuals, to name only a few. Right now we're Rockin' the Casbah,[8] but at the end of the day All You Need Is Love,[9] so start by learning to love yourself and to Love the One You're With.[10] Then, and only then, can we truly start to stand united and break the chains of our past.

As Lenny Kravitz (via Yogi Berra) sings, "It ain't over till it's over,"[11] so if you're feeling stuck in a Nick at Nite *M*A*S*H* marathon loop, it's time to pull the plug, launch Operation Open Heart, and stop history from repeating itself once and for all.

For Weddings
and a Funeral

May 3, 2011

I tried to resist, I really did. I did not want to contribute one
more thought to the nuptials of two young royals, a story
that has been regurgitated, dissected and discussed in a
plethora of ways ad nauseam for the months, weeks and
days leading to it. And once it was officially over, we hoped
we could move on with more important things, and I don't
mean birth certificates or transcripts.

But then a funny thing happened. Having a minor curiosity
in the whole affair, I woke up Friday morning, turned on the
TV, and like the tornadoes that had devastatingly destroyed
much of Alabama the day before, I somehow got sucked
into the vortex of everything Wills and Kate!! It was hard to
get around it, frankly, and like that darn car accident everyone slows down for, I simply could not turn away.

Besides getting the dress fix, I was mesmerized by the
orderliness of the mega-crowd; the sheer detail, beauty and
majesty of it all, and how much global attention had been
placed on this singular event, which unified a nation and
the world. I thought about how people can indeed come
together in positive, dare I say, innocent ways, even if much
of it comes down to a shared fantasy. And then another
funny thing happened.

In the midst of writing this, news broke of the demise of a man with a turban and beard who had ties to a different royal family, and many people all around our country gathered spontaneously in the streets to revel in the news. This received equal if not more global attention, but how jubilant an occasion is it really? Significant and somber, yes, but having a party to celebrate revenge and the death of anyone is not the same. No matter how happy you are that Bin Laden is dead, that type of celebration comes from a place of hate and fear, not love.

My writing often encourages you to **Let Love Rule**, because What the World Needs Now Is Love,[12] sweet love. Fairy tales and fascination aside, no matter who you are, what you look like, or where you come from, we all want to love and be loved in return. Even with bad decisions and family feuds, weddings are generally joyous occasions and funerals are not, but both tap into our desire for that most basic of human needs and should always unify us for good.

You may live in Queens or in Kings County, but you don't have to come from a special bloodline or marry a prince or princess to have a charmed life; just become the sovereign monarch of your own peaceful kingdom and love life happily ever after!

Battle of the Bulge

June 14, 2011

Last week my relative from Argentina couldn't get here due to the fallout from a major volcanic eruption in Chile that kept flights from leaving Buenos Aires—it was so massive it was affecting air travel as far away as Australia! Iceland recently experienced a volcanic eruption as well, though not quite as disruptive as last year's. Arizona and Southern Colorado are on fire, and not in the "cool" way, massacres and secret wars are happening in the Middle East, the economy is imploding ... but you wouldn't know what was really going on these days from watching the news.

There is no doubt that sex sells, but at what price to our dignity and destiny as individuals and as a country? The media blitz about a certain congressman with an unfortunate surname to match his predicament clouded the media landscape to the point that we could not seem to find out much else—except perhaps the hot air being blown about by a former governor from Alaska, with her accounts of American history, the news of her old emails, or her lunch with a certain NYC "landmark" with bad hair.

In the famous WWII battle, which was one of the Nazis' biggest attacks on Allied forces, particularly the Americans, Hitler's divide-and-conquer strategy was helped by the weather—actual fog—that settled in for two days, grounding the Allies' superior air power and the reason we suffered greatly at the time.

Besides the literal wars currently taking place across the globe, we are experiencing a war over our minds and hearts, about what merits discussion and analysis and what is simply gossip. It's easy to get sucked into whatever the media is doing to grab our attention, so we must fight to separate the wheat from the chaff in every area of our lives, redirecting our focus to something more productive and meaningful.

Summer is a perfect time to expand your horizons, travel and explore. But if you can't physically make a journey, there is always dance, art, literature and learning about other people's realities—not from a "reality" TV show, but through documentaries like those shown at the annual Human Rights Watch Film Festival.

Can't quite discern what the fog is concealing, the volcanic ash is covering up, or those smoke signals are trying to warn you about? Break through the distractions that block you from dealing with the important stuff in your life and the world at large, because it's only On a Clear Day[13] when you can see what's going on within and around you, so you can keep on reachin' for that Higher Ground![14]

Follow the Leader

September 20, 2011

The time of year is once again upon us when leaders from all sectors and nations around the globe descend on New York City. Along with street closings and traffic jams, they come together to make important speeches, hold panel discussions, and attend fancy galas.

Between the UN General Assembly, the Clinton Global Initiative, two major women's conferences and other events, all these bigwigs and accomplished folks will be setting out to solve the world's problems with a whirlwind of high-level networking and powwows throughout the week. Boy, do they have their hands full!

This month, *Vanity Fair* features its list of the 2011 New Establishment, along with the old and some hall of famers to boot, many of whom will surely be in town. Most are from technology and media, which shows you where all the power currently lies, not to mention the vast majority are men—but these are topics for another time ...

So how did these people in government, corporations, NGOs, technology, media and more become the leaders they are today? My guess is that they took hold of their passion, their calling in life, and harnessed it in a way that led them wherever it needed to go.

Not all the journeys were the same; I'm sure some worked very hard for a long time with their eyes on the prize, others became leaders by accident due to some circumstance that thrust them into the spotlight, and many were born at the right place at the right time and seized the opportunity to make their mark on the world. They all had to have lots of help along the way, and regardless of how they arrived, at some point they had to own the fact that they did.

But keep in mind that they are no different from you and me. We are all made of the same biological substance, and at the end of the day, as the saying goes, they put their pants on one leg at time, which means any one of us has the opportunity to be a leader in some way, shape or form. In fact, we can and must be the leaders in our own lives if we are to have any hope or effectiveness at leading others, either directly or by example.

Tomorrow happens to be the International Day of Peace and as I frequently say (see **Joni Mitchell Never Lies** and **Peas on Earth**), we are all responsible for creating peace in our piece of the pie. So why not ask yourself: Am I leading the life I want to live? If you were in the running for a little gold statuette, would you be in the leading lady/man category in your own best drama or comedy, in a supporting role, or an extra left on the cutting room floor?

Feeling like you're spinning in circles or vetoed at every turn these days? Whether a paparazzi-deprived/ambushed star or not, someone has to lead in the dance of your life, and the only person to do that is you. So get out there with the focus and direction you need to express your true power and potential, and that will put you at the top of the leaderboard on your own world stage!

A Tale of Two Streets

October 18, 2011

Whether you think we are living in the best of times or the worst, they certainly are *interesting* times.

I assure you that I am very much part of the 99 percent being represented in Zuccotti Park, and now all around the world. I stand with the Occupy Wall Street movement insofar as it is protesting greed and corruption, which is a misuse of power in the area of money; but it's important to remember that money itself did not cause the problem.

Fighting to bring justice to those who have gotten away with crime and to help those who are suffering because of it is one thing; hating all people who have money, even those who earned it with integrity and hard work, does not make sense. It doesn't even make sense to hate the system that allowed it to happen; it's *people* who abused and twisted the system to their advantage.

I love money. It took me a long time to understand and be comfortable saying that because of all the connotations, including the school of thought that espouses "money is evil" and "rich people are bad." But I know I have my priorities straight and I've come to see money as something I strive to have a healthy and balanced relationship with; therefore if I want to have more of it, I have to love and respect it so it can treat me right. If I hated money, why would money come into my life?

I also know that money isn't the end, it's simply the means, and I've only ever given it supporting-role status in my life, never the be-all and end-all of my existence. (Just ask my friends and family who have witnessed my journey these past 10 years!) Money is an energy, and like any other type of energy, it's how you use it that counts. I am still learning, but because of the choices I have made and the extremes I have experienced, I have come to a Zen place with it, at least for now.

The necessity of money in our lives is a reality that is not going away any time soon, if ever, and changing the ways we exchange goods and services or govern ourselves won't make much of a difference if people themselves don't change.

As I say in all my seminars, at the end of the day, you need to define what prosperity means for *you* in all aspects of life. You must know that you are not your bank account, and that your self-worth and happiness are not determined by your salary or your stuff.

Wondering how you can get from being a have-not to having a life that is affluent in mind, body and spirit? Determine what wealth means to you, and you can begin your journey from rags to riches, pauper to prince(ss), creating an earthly experience filled with purpose and meaning that surpasses all the Great Expectations you could ever have!

American Horror Story

October 25, 2011

Halloween *used* to be one of, if not my favorite holidays. Costumes, parties, piles of candy not normally allowed in the house (Choco'Lites were the best!), collecting pennies in my orange UNICEF box ... As a young adult, it became more about creating unique/clever ensembles from thrift stores or scratch, then later marching in the Village Halloween Parade years before it became the monstrosity (pun intended) it is today. No matter what, it was always good clean fun.

The past several years, at least in NYC, there's been an explosion of Halloween hacks (pun intended again). Like so many other things, it's been commercialized ad nauseam, with store-bought costumes (a Ricky's on every corner, it seems), mostly slutty versions of professions, or zombies, and it's become an excuse to black out from drinking, not an opportunity for creativity, imagination and humor.

It used to be that a small crop of horror flicks would came out around this time (and a few in the summer) with fellas named Michael, Freddy, Jason and Chucky. Now it's year-round vampires, witches, werewolves, haunted houses, and a host of other things that are sick, twisted and go more-than-bump in the night on TV/cable or the big screen, not to mention video games that take violence in general to a whole other level—all of which further desensitizes us to brutal attacks both at home and abroad.

What if instead we took the best of other holidays (Thanksgiving, Christmas, Valentine's Day, even Fourth of July!)—with as many secular, feel-good themes and positive sentiments that abound—and spread *that* 24/7? There's enough negativity and fear to deal with in the reality of our everyday lives, so wouldn't it be nice to bombard ourselves year-round with the uplifting and leave the scary/slasher stuff to just a few weeks prior to October 31?

The good news is you have a choice in what you let sink into your brain cells. I choose to acknowledge the dark side yet turn the other way, put on some shades and counteract the sinister with sunshine, and I hope that reflects back to make a brighter, lighter world, at least in my neck of the woods.

Need a one-way ticket out of Spookytown to experience a more "normal" type of activity in and around your abode? Heed those childhood warnings and avoid the Stranger or anything that will make you Scream, so you can gain confidence and become stronger in mind, body and spirit to you can take on any trick, and enjoy plenty of treats instead!

Peas on Earth

December 20, 2011

Well, it was a bad year for dictators, and that's a good thing for the rest of us. Now that there is the possibility, and in fact the dawning or rebirth of a more democratic existence across the globe, we must remember to do our part to make it so.

No matter what the topic, I always talk about two things in my seminars: how can we expect to have peace on this planet if we don't have peace in our own lives; and everyone should cook. Ergo, we must have peace in our kitchens in order to have peace in our lives in order to have peace in the world.

Whether you consider yourself the next Top Chef or think heating up leftovers in the microwave qualifies, my go-to recipe that gourmets and gauche gourmands alike can make is pea soup. Cooking in general, and especially something like soup, is extremely meditative and teaches us that life does not always function like an instant message. It forces you to slow down, be more present, have more patience, and then enjoy the fruits of your labor.

One ingredient alone won't cut it, and you can really make the recipe your own. Each chopped-up piece of onion, carrot, celery, garlic (ham, kale, turnip, parsnip, sweet potato ... whatever else you want to put in there), and of course split peas, ultimately blends together in a harmonious way; the whole meal is highly nutritious with many healthy benefits, and the subtle combination of these diverse components brings out the best, over time, in every ingredient. Yum.

The United States has been called a melting pot, and as a struggling global superpower, if that can truly be realized in its most positive sense, the rest of the world has a pretty good shot as well. So as you're making the soup, perhaps visualize the ingredients as red states and blue states, the rich and the poor, white, black, Muslim, non-Muslim, gay, straight, liberal and conservative—and why not throw in the countries of the European Union as well, since they need all the help they can get at the moment ...

But if you really are a menace in the galley, you can always take a mental ride on the Peace Train[15] or imagine yourself as a member of the YouTube Symphony Orchestra, with 100 artists from over 30 countries playing more than two dozen diverse instruments, coming together to create that beautiful universal language known as music.

Still feel as though your Jong is kind of Il? Boil down your focus to uniting your body, relationships, career and life so they can be peas in a pod, allowing you to experience a deeper sense of peace in your piece of the pie.

World Wide Web

November 6, 2012

The Saturday before Superstorm Sandy, I was at a Halloween party. The host went to town with decorations and had massive floor-to-ceiling spider webs in several corners. Little did I know what foreshadowing that would be for the week ahead!

Four years ago this week, we were on the eve of a historic presidential election, after a historic financial disaster. That Fall, the unimaginable became imaginable on both fronts when we chose our first black president and watched the implosion of the stock market and our banking system. This woke us up in more ways than one, and both divided and connected us.

Fast-forward to today, and we are on the eve of yet another historic election, the outcome yet to be determined, and post another disaster, this time a natural one, which is hitting us materially as much as anything else. And we are even more divided, yet more connected than ever.

After the financial crisis of 2008, because of the actions of a relative few that rippled throughout the world, at the very least we were forced to deal with our addiction to credit and consumerism, and at the worst lost our homes and jobs because of it. Now it's Mother Nature aided by the man-made contribution to/ignorance of climate change teaching us that lesson with a more visceral punch as we recover from power outages and gas shortages at the least, and physical destruction of our property and loss of life at the worst.

Since this hit the tri-state area, because of its special density of population and unique connection to the global as well as local economy, no one is exempt from this lesson; everyone has been affected in one way or another—it's just who, what, when, where, how and level of gravity that varies.

In the middle of the storm, the facade of an apartment building in Chelsea was ripped off, showing a dollhouse-like view of the inside, a symbolic representation of what is happening to us physically and emotionally as the walls and structures between and around us are being torn down in order to reveal the truth of our lives.

Our interconnectedness and vulnerability have been thrown in our face—not only through weather, power, gas, goods and services, transportation and social media, but relationally too. How long can you coexist in the disconnected dark, live back at Mom's, stay at your friend's, or sleep with strangers at a shelter 24/7? How many days can you work from home, or miss work altogether, or have three-hour commutes, or wait hours in line for gas without losing it? Community is a funny thing in New York—we like the anonymity and self-sufficiency of living on top of each other and the illusion of togetherness that brings, but actually having to interact and be with each other and ask for or receive help is another story.

People have mentioned how Sandy is too "nice" a moniker

for what she did, but just like the gentle soul of Franken-stein for which she was also named, there is goodness to be found underneath the external horror of her monstrous appearance. She is asking us to come together like never before and question the deepest meaning of our lives; she is forcing us not only to realize but to actually *experience* the ways we are now more connected than ever, more interdependent than at any other time in history. And it is a gift because experience is usually the only way we humans learn, and that, as painful as it may be, is something to be grateful for if we choose to accept it as such.

Like big elections, these are the occasions when we focus passionately on something that impacts us all; they bring out the best and worst in us. We get to see people's true colors, good, bad or indifferent; how flexible we can be; how generous and open-hearted we are; and how we distill down what is vitally important, what is a necessity and what is merely a luxury—or when suddenly those necessities become luxuries after not having them for a few days. Such events test our patience, politeness, perseverance and willingness to exist in the present. They also show us the incredible strength and spirit of humanity, our willingness to help one another, our capacity for leadership and organization, and our ability to rise to the occasion in times of crisis.

So remember, when we wake up tomorrow morning, no matter what the result of this election is, and no matter where we live in this country or on this planet, what we know for sure, now more than ever, is that we are all in this together.

Get Up, Stand Up

July 9, 2013

One of the things I try to do when speaking to groups in career transition is put the power back in their hands and their hearts. I let you know that you should not accept your fate as victims of a system or think you are subject to the whims of the economy, conventional wisdom, how things appear on the surface, or any external voices—and that where there is a will there is a way.

I want you to find the connection, strength and truth of who you are and how you got to this moment, then motivate you to make the changes necessary to grow and move forward in a positive direction in your career and life. I ask you to take back control of your job search, trust in the process, and often end in a half-joking way with my fist up and the rally cry, Power to the People![16]

It's not that I ignore the cold, hard reality of the way the world works these days and how that might impact job prospects or a fulfilling existence, but I do want to wake folks up to the fact that they are not passive participants in life and that they have much more power over and responsibility for their situation than they might realize or want to admit. Which means they can't blame anyone, and they probably just have to work a little harder or smarter to get the results they want.

We've collectively come to a crossroads where this could not be more true; we've allowed a variety of entities to take over, bombard and bamboozle our hearts, minds and bodies—whether governments, corporations, the military, Hollywood, or some combination of them all—and take advantage of our numbing tendencies, heads in the sand, electronic distractions, or sheer need to survive the daily grind ... how much longer can we take it?

With all the recent talk about spying, why not do some internal surveillance to observe and feel what's going on in your life right now. What kind of tyranny is dictating your thoughts, words and deeds, consciously or subconsciously? Where can you take action, even if only symbolic, to show that you, not your oppressor, is in charge? What is your version of Tahrir, Taksim or Brasilia? What would Edith Windsor, Wendy Davis or Tim DeChristopher do in your situation? What Supreme Court judgments do you need to overturn or restore in your heart? How can you bend the rules in your favor without breaking them, or engage in civil disobedience when the rules are no longer (or never were) valid or have become corrupted? Where do you need more courage in your life? What can you liberate yourself from?

As I always say, personal transformation is the key to social transformation, so if we want a better world we need to start with our own. Use that intelligence gathering to find something, someone, or some idea in your life that is holding you back—keeping in mind that this is often your own ego or limiting beliefs! Perhaps it's simply letting go of the image of who you think you are supposed to be or were told you are, or maybe it's approaching a health issue, relationship or unemployment with forgiveness and a new point of view that puts you in the driver's seat. Or maybe the most radical thing you can do is love yourself unconditionally.

Need a little help Shaking the Tree?[17] Dig deep and find the Strength, Courage and Wisdom[18] to Use the Force[19] and create the life you so deserve!

All Roads: Same Place

September 25, 2013

September is always an exciting time of year for me as world leaders convene on the island of Manhattan for the United Nations General Assembly and the Clinton Global Initiative.

Many of you know my degree is in International Relations. Early on I was a passionate student of languages and cultures, and was bitten by the travel bug at age 12 after a trip to Spain, Portugal and Morocco with my grandmother. By senior year in high school I was studying Spanish, French and Italian (forgoing chemistry and physics ...), and in college I took Mandarin Chinese, organized international student orientations, studied abroad ... you get the picture.

My dream was to one day work for the UN, as my intention and mission in life was to contribute to world peace (I simply didn't understand why people and countries couldn't get along just because of race, religion, or anything else), so that was a seemingly logical goal. Who grows up wanting to be a career/life coach? Like so many professions today, that didn't even exist when I was a kid! Ah, but the Universe has a funny way of working things out.

Once I discovered that being employed by the UN did not ultimately fit my skill set or desired environment, I set out to create my own international experiences—teaching middle and high school Spanish, working and traveling with an upscale educational tour operator, teaching Tourism Destinations and Cultures at NYU, and founding my own mini-version of the UN called The Women's Mosaic, which brings together women from different cultures and backgrounds to learn from and be inspired by one another.

As a result of that creation, I got hooked into the UN; met several times and received praise from Kofi Annan; have attended many of its conferences (I still get verklempt when I am in the auditorium wearing an earpiece ...); and before any of this, without consciously trying, ended up living in the very neighborhood where the UN headquarters is situated! So for my entire adult life, I have been surrounded by diplomats and their missions, sharing my coffee shop, gym and grocery store with them 24/7.

Fast-forward to more recently, as my interest and passion for personal growth, empowerment and healing, along with my ability to relate to just about anyone, combined with x-ray vision, supersonic hearing, and a broad knowledge of industries, careers and other resources have united to make me into this very interesting and profoundly effective person I will call a career/life coach, for lack of a better title. And I have been helping people professionally in this capacity for over six years.

Last week I had a big "aha moment" after a Skype session with a new client in Hungary who had attended one of my talks while here on holiday. Although that was only my second international call, I realized just how diverse and, yes, *global* my clientele is! I have worked with well over a hundred people from all backgrounds—whether foreign nationals visiting or working here temporarily, or folks who came to live here as children or adults. They hail from Macedonia, Italy, Puerto Rico, Mexico, New Zealand, Dominican Republic, China, Taiwan, Nigeria, Canada, Australia, El Salvador, Russia, Japan, Philippines and Israel, and they embody the many diverse ethnicities and religions found here—African-American, Haitian, Indian, Persian, Muslim, Jewish, Buddhist, Quaker and so much more; many of my clients have accents because English is their second or *third* language! So DUH, here I am using my degree in international relations yet once again, simply in another form. Pretty cool, huh?

I share all of this not just to illustrate how the thread of my interests and passions have run through everything I do, but also for this: My work with individuals only confirms my theories, thoughts and ideals about countries and humanity as a whole. The more I learn and intimately observe the intricacies of all these *seemingly* different folks' journeys and backgrounds, the more I see the hard evidence of how we are all wired with the same desires, dreams, hopes and challenges. No matter what corner of the globe we are from, we have far more in common than you can imagine.

Think you're so special? You are. You have a uniqueness that you bring to this planet. But you are also made of the same stuff as that guy or gal across the ocean or sitting next to you on the subway. And because of things like technology and climate change, we are more interconnected than ever. So this week, take a moment to expand your horizons: Who can you learn about, chat with, or help in some way that is out of your normal sphere of influence? How can you Imagine[20] your world for the better? What can you do to think globally but act locally?

Not sure how the micro in your life will affect the macro? Maybe you need someone, perhaps even me, to help you translate the language of your soul to see how it will weave into the tapestry of history and become that much-needed piece of the peace puzzle we are all a part of, no matter who you are or where you come from.

You Say You Want a Revolution

December 11, 2013

One of the things I learned when I was negotiating was that until I changed myself, I could not change others.
—Nelson Mandela

Revolution is the evolution of humans into a higher humanity.
—Grace Lee Boggs

Those of you who know me or who read these posts are aware that my passion and mission in life has always been to contribute to world peace, mostly through my work, best expressed in my mantra that personal transformation is the key to social transformation.

So it should come as no surprise that I profoundly relate to and revere the lives of these two nonagenarians, Nelson Mandela, who died last week at age 95, and 98-year-old activist and author Grace Lee Boggs. They literally embody this philosophy in every cell of their beings; they have demonstrated it externally with their activism and sacrifice for racial equality and social justice, and internally by the wisdom they have gained and generously share from nearly a century of experience, observation and, most important, reflection.

Both started out as "radicals" and were branded as terrorists with the requisite FBI/CIA files (Mandela was even on the US terrorism watch list until 2008!) because they initially saw the only way to overthrow the entrenched power structure was by employing the more literal and sometimes violent tactics of revolution through organized movements and a spirit of rebellion. But through trial and error, incarceration, and maturity, they eventually evolved; they gave themselves permission to change their minds, learn, and grow in light of new information, experimentation and, once again, reflection—ultimately coming to the conclusion that in order to change the world, they would have to change themselves.

They came to understand that humanity is indeed made up of humans and that humans were going to have to deal with other humans in order to get anything done. So we'd better be the best we can be as individuals and try to get along and get past our differences and disagreements, because the reality is we must coexist harmoniously—whether in a racially divided African country, a rundown bankrupt American city, or in our very own household.

We are living in extraordinary times, and it is no accident that you are who you are at this moment in history.

What does your humanity mean to you? As our world continues to go through turbulent changes and upheavals, it will be up to us individually and collectively to do our part to "tear down" where necessary and rebuild a more enlightened society that reflects our *evolved* humanity.

But we have to start with ourselves and do what we can in our immediate environments to demonstrate our own evolution—which, by the way, does not happen overnight or with a magic pill, silver bullet, or special app.

Only through keen observation, deep reflection, and inner and outer sweating effort and energy over a long period of time directed toward improving ourselves and serving others can true transformation take place. Then if we're lucky, by the time we reach our 90s, we can look back and see how our journey has positively and productively unfolded in both a personal and political way, and be proud of what we accomplished and the legacy we will leave behind.

Wondering how it will all go down if *you* take up the cause? Then maybe it's time to incite a riot in your heart so you can make the most of what you've got, and at the end of the day know it's gonna be all right![3]

They Might Be Giants

June 4, 2014

If a human being dreams a great dream, dares to love someone. ... If a human being dares to be bigger than the condition into which she or he was born, it means so can you. ... I am a human being, nothing human can be alien to me. —Maya Angelou

And what a human she was! Dr. Maya Angelou possessed and cultivated a creative and brilliant mind, a powerful and compassionate heart, a flair for the dramatic, a serious sense of humor, and a thorough appetite for all aspects of life. She was a phenomenal woman who spent every breath of her 86 years consciously striving to express the fullest embodiment of what it means to exist as a spiritual being in this physical world.

To me, this is her greatest legacy. Like my other six-foot-tall heroine, Eleanor Roosevelt, she walked her talk and therefore we all benefited. She served as an example for all she stood for and knew to be Universally true; she espoused the unity and dignity of people of every race and creed, recognizing that "we are more alike than we are unalike."

And she was very aware that she was indeed human, and she knew how dangerous it is to make people like Martin Luther King Jr., Gandhi or Mother Teresa larger than life— they were all human beings and when we idolize or put them on a pedestal, they become inaccessible and we think we can never be like them. Instead, they should inspire us to be extraordinary in our own way.

In our youth-obsessed and advertising-driven culture, it is unfortunate that we give so little airtime to our elders like Dr. Angelou, Nelson Mandela or Grace Lee Boggs (see **You Say You Want a Revolution**), because when we listen to the wisdom that nearly nine decades of being people who have chosen to love, forgive, learn and grow, who allowed them-selves to reflect, observe and evolve, *they teach us how to live*. They are lighthouses that remind us who we really are and where we should be going—and these days especially, when one is extinguished it feels like an even bigger loss because they are rare gems and we wonder who is coming up to replace them.

In my work I have the honor and privilege of helping you discover that no matter how old you are or where you are from, you have a unique way of leaving our planet a little better off than when you arrived—even if it is simply by virtue of your own healed life.

Some of my clients, as a result of our meeting, have already gone on to win Tonys and Fulbrights, or are on their way to becoming media moguls, best-selling authors, cutting-edge inventors, or warriors for justice; whether they have an Ivy League background, were formerly incarcerated, or are a ninth-grade NYC public school student (see **Life Class**), every one of them has something to offer, an opportunity to improve their own world, a way to be the most human they can be.

Not quite convinced that you too can be a giant among us? Like those redwoods of California, you are one of hundreds of special trees that make up a forest of awe-inspiring majesty and beauty, living in harmony with one another and Earth, and the very nature of Life itself.

Beauty & the Beast

August 20, 2014

The past few weeks have been ugly.

Tragic and senseless death and destruction both here and abroad feel like yet another punch in the stomach. We've been trying to find some solid ground to get our breathing back to normal after the wind has been knocked out of us repeatedly, as we react with shock and dismay to countless horror stories and history repeating itself streaming at us from every which way.

If, like me, you are a sensitive person, you found that your equilibrium has been a little off, that there has been a disturbance in the Force, a cosmic warp in the Universe that came with a collective sigh, utter frustration, and profound sadness on many levels, for a variety of reasons.

That's the bad news.

The last few weeks have also brought us some of the most gorgeous summer weather the East Coast has had in years, and we've seen a multitude of people pouring buckets of ice water over their heads for a good cause—mostly to make us laugh—simultaneously counteracting all the less-than-humorous happenings. And in my own sphere, I have been fortunate to visit some picture-perfect places, reconnect with old friends, make progress on several longtime goals, and celebrate tremendous transformation in my clients, which makes me love what I do even more and gives me a deep sense of satisfaction and joy like no other.

That's the sort-of good news. Because these days, it seems that ugly is the status quo. We are bombarded with so many negative events, factual and fictional—served up as entertainment—that we have simply become used to it. In these days of doom and gloom, I encourage you all to imagine the opposite: What if Beauty became the norm?

And when I talk about Beauty, I don't mean a two-dimensional feast for the eyes, or pleasure for pleasure's sake, although that is part of it. True beauty is three-dimensional; it is something to be *felt* and *experienced*, not just superficially appreciated. Beauty happens inside *and* out. It is never just cosmetic. It is something to be absorbed by every fiber of your being, whether admiring a work of art, listening to music, observing Nature in its magnificent glory, witnessing an act of courage or compassion, or enjoying a person's human expression at its best.

So where do we begin? How do we do this? It's tempting to just tune out and distract ourselves with whatever we can and hope that the problems of the world instantly vanish or that some drug company creates a pill for peace. But the truth is that the more disconnected and desensitized we become, the more problems we will have. Most people are walking around emotionally constipated. We need to keep our senses alive, intact, ebbing and flowing in a balanced way—yet not letting them run the show or allowing any external images or situations to grab control of us. We need to be able to respond from the deepest human level so we can know how to react, when to take action, when to pick up the phone, when to tweet or post something, when to set boundaries or ask for help, or when to turn off the TV or computer.

Brené Brown, in her now-famous Ted Talk on vulnerability, tells us that when we numb the bad, we numb the good too. So we can't just shut ourselves off if we want to feel love, compassion, empathy, kindness—or yes, even feel beauty. *Feeling means we are alive.* If not, then what are we?

Duality is a fact of life: in order to appreciate the sunshine, you need the rain.[21] Once you are able to connect with and feel ALL of what is going on within you, with a little regular detox of laughter and tears, you can deal with the not-so-pleasant emotions as they come up, let go of them more easily, and conversely take hold of and relish in the positive, ecstatic and joyous ones even longer—expanding and benefiting from that energy more profoundly.

Look for Beauty everywhere and let in the Beauty to overpower the beast. Allow the darkness, anger, pain and shame to move through you so that you can then use that same vehicle to embody and express supreme joy and love when they abound. You can then more accurately observe and call out injustice because you know in your heart what truth, justice, goodness and beauty *look* and *feel* like.

Not quite sure how to go from Blah to Bliss? Be sure to stop and smell the roses because living life as a full-fledged member of the human race has its rewards, and being able to FEEL Truth, Freedom, Beauty and Love are by far the best.

Grown-Ups

September 25, 2014

The mark of the immature man is that he wants to die nobly for a cause, while the mark of the mature man is that he wants to live humbly for one.
—J.D. Salinger, *The Catcher in the Rye*

Most people don't grow up. Most people age. They find parking spaces, honor their credit cards, get married, have children, and call that maturity. What that is, is aging.
—Maya Angelou

Growing up is hard, love. Otherwise everyone would do it.
—Kim Harrison, *Pale Demon*

With the International Day of Peace, People's Climate March, UN General Assembly, Clinton Global Initiative and Global Citizen Festival culminating this week, the spotlight has been on our responsibility as nations and citizens to take care of each other and this planet we inhabit.

But all too often it seems the remaining 51 weeks of the year we forget that we have any say or power or control over our lives and environment as we are lulled back into our daily routines—Mother Nature has her way with us; radical terrorists and out-of-control law enforcement use violence in extreme ways to threaten us physically and psychologically here and abroad; our government legislates what we should eat, think and do with our bodies; and corporations use advertising, lobbying and Hollywood to tell us who we are, what we should buy, believe in, and vote for, and what we should or should not be doing with our time, money and energy.

And in our private lives, we tend to rely on others—whether parents, spouses and partners, friends, doctors, teachers, bosses, news outlets or conventional wisdom—more than we should, and we are more overwhelmed and distracted than ever by digital media via accompanying gadgets/appendages. As a result, we forget we can have a unique opinion, make more conscious decisions that go against the grain, and above all think for ourselves rather than just absorb and digest (literally and metaphorically) what is being offered, served or shoved down our throats.

When you're a child, you generally have no choice or don't know better and have to accept the status quo of whatever the adults around you say goes, but as you get older it's time to check in and ask yourself, Who's Your Daddy now?

Relationships are the glue that holds the world together and gives meaning to our lives; they include our relationship to ourselves, each other, our country, the Earth, and the Universe/God/Higher Power/Nature. But when we allow a relationship to anyone or anything outside ourselves to be the ultimate authority over us—whether with a parent, child, friend, the government, social media or zeitgeist—we are giving up our individual power to control our destiny and preventing ourselves from emotionally maturing. These are the types of unhealthy dependent relationships, rather than healthy *inter*dependent ones, that are causing our planet to fall apart.

Growing up means taking responsibility for every aspect of your life. Many of us prefer to remain in a half-baked adulthood that never really evolves to its full potential because we are too busy or distracted to see who is really in control—and because it's easier to pop a pill or let someone else take care of it. But it requires courage, elbow grease, and internal effort every step of the way to be who we are truly meant to be.

We all have to do our part to take ownership of our environment, health and happiness in mind, body and spirit. *No one else can do this for us.* By becoming stronger in who you are, you can then use your full power and potential to help those who cannot yet help themselves, and create structures and systems from microcosm to macrocosm that will support a sustainable and peaceful life, no matter who you are or where you are from.

Still feeling like a Toys"R"Us kid? We need you to mature into a full-fledged self-mama or self-papa (without losing that essential childlike sense of play!) so that we can create a global village of audacious, authentic adults.

LOVE

Let Love Rule

September 28, 2010

Last week, New York City was buzzing with world leaders and dignitaries clogging traffic and attending the UN General Assembly, where they came together to solve issues relating to peace and poverty.

When Lenny Kravitz came out with his anthem[1] in 1989, the world was at once very different from and exactly the same as it is now. The Cold War has been replaced by the War on Terror, the Middle East remains a mess, and there are still far too many people on the planet who live in the midst of hunger, disease and injustice. Racism and religious bigotry are alive and well, and economies and the environment are in the tank. Heavy sigh ... when will we ever learn?

So what is little ole you to do? Well if, as the saying goes, peace begins with me, then the question is, Are you at war with yourself or with the people closest to you?

A loving relationship with yourself must come before you can be in one with another, or even just to get along with your family, neighbors or strangers on the subway. We have to take the time and energy to forgive and love ourselves and others. It's our responsibility to dig deep to see what's going on inside us, understand it, and have the courage to communicate honestly and lovingly first to ourselves, then to those around us when appropriate.

Love is the most powerful force in the Universe when used intelligently and intentionally; it can move mountains, heal, connect and transform.

What are you waiting for? There is no more important time than *now* to let love start ruling your world. Love of yourself, love of each other, love of your work, and love of life itself— the very breath and heartbeat that is allowing you to read this!

Are you in need of a little mediation between your head and your heart, what you earn and what you're worth, your desires and your reality, or you and your significant other? Make love the law of the land; it will be the peacekeeping force that helps you reconcile all the conflict zones in your life ...

Free Love

Independence Day is one of my favorite holidays for a variety of reasons, and not just for the day off, barbecues and fireworks. America's birthday holds a special place in my heart for the idealism it inspires and the respect and gratitude I have for the wisdom, sacrifice and, most of all, courage that our Founding Fathers displayed that fateful summer of 1776.

As I always mention in my seminars, the root of the word courage is *cor*, the Latin word for heart. This means that anything requiring courage is something that comes from the heart, from a place of deep love, a passion for what one is pushing oneself to do.

The Founding Fathers' profound love for Life, Liberty and Justice laid the foundation for the birth of a nation that promotes the growth of its most precious natural resource— the freedom of its citizens, i.e., *We the People*—to use our time and energy as we see fit, expressing ourselves and living a life we choose that is without harm to others. Because of the diversity of the 13 colonies, each with its own interests and identity, the ideal at the time had to be compromised regarding the institution of slavery in order to gain a unanimous vote for independence from England. ... But we had to start somewhere, otherwise we might really have been affected by Kate and Will's nuptials across the pond, or all our TV hosts would be British ... oh wait ...

Our country is by no means perfect and will continue to have its ups and downs, but ultimately it's up to each of us to make it the best we can. So what will your contribution be to this great experiment? How will you leave your symbolic "John Hancock" on history?

One thing we can all do is make the question "Where Is the Love?"[2] obsolete in our corner of the world. Each of us can exercise that freedom 24/7, so be sure to consistently unleash your love on that special someone, your work, your friends and family, your community, a cause, the nation, the planet, strangers, and life itself.

You say you want a Revolution?[3] Go ahead and ring the Liberty Bell in your life because we are all Free to Be ... You and Me.[4]

Just Desserts

March 20, 2012

Justice is what love looks like in public, just like tenderness is what love feels like in private. —Cornel West

Be kind; everyone you meet is fighting a hard battle.
—Ian MacLaren

I'm a pretty even-keeled gal and have become somewhat adept at managing/mitigating stress in my life, the techniques of which I share with others through my work. Part of that strategy includes limiting/filtering my daily dose of news and media so as not to be overwhelmed by the gloom and doom that is the majority of what is broadcast.

But lately I've been feeling like the character in that famous scene from the 1976 movie *Network*: "I'm as mad as hell and I'm not gonna take this anymore!" Just pick a topic, whether our broken political system, the war on women's reproductive health, the global economic mess and decline of the middle class, or vigilantes and blatant attacks both here and abroad—including massacres and ethnic cleansing, both overt and subtle, of particular races, religions, sexual orientations and nations. So many things are under siege in our culture, in society and around the world that it's easy to be lulled into the feeling that we can't do anything. But we can take matters into our hands—in a responsible way.

Besides using our voice, signature and/or pocketbook to make a difference, we can check our egos at the door and let balanced emotions, not uncontrolled rage or fear, guide our actions. There are plenty of wonky/intellectual and pseudo-intellectual approaches to go around and also, unfortunately, pure hatred and insanity to fuel many an action, so the question that we all need to answer is: How can we inject more love, understanding and compassion in order to effect the change we want?

A good place to begin is to think about how we can create more justice and peace in our own lives, starting with our relationships. Are you unfairly punishing, harshly judging or incorrectly perceiving people closest to you, whether family, friends or those you work with? Are the thoughts and actions toward yourself and others around you positive and constructive, or negative and destructive?

Since today is the first day of Spring, it's a good time to clean out our mental and emotional closets, in addition to our physical ones. By making more of a commitment to create our own just and peaceful world, only then can we expect it of the world around us. 'Cause guess what? That world is made of us!

Do what you can to activate love and compassion within you, scan reactions and prejudices, don't throw stones, and stand up for those who can't. Most of all, go easy on yourself! We're often our own worst critics and judges, and we end up imprisoning ourselves and those around us because of it. Most people are doing the best they can. As so eloquently stated in a TED Talk by Bryan Stevenson, remember that "each of us is more than the worst thing we've ever done" and "ultimately, our humanity depends on everyone's humanity."

Not quite sure where you need to balance the scales of justice in your life? Find someone, perhaps even me, who can be a softer, gentler version of Judge Judy, helping you to separate fact from fiction in your court of personal opinion so you can spring yourself from whatever slammer you've locked yourself in.

All That You Can't Leave Behind

April 3, 2012

I recently attended the funeral of a good friend's father. He was Ukrainian, along with most of his relatives and friends, so everything was conducted in his native language. At the brunch after the burial, a woman stood up and read with great emotion what she had written on a few sheets of loose-leaf paper while many of us choked up.

I saw her by the ladies' room soon after and mentioned how beautiful her speech was. In broken English, she went on about how she messed up and it didn't come out the way she wanted, etc. I stopped her midsentence and said, "I don't speak a word of Ukrainian." Puzzled, she replied, "Well, I just spoke from my heart." And I said, "Yes, that's why it was so beautiful."

I often begin my seminars reminding the attendees that someday, hopefully in the very distant future, they will die. Perhaps it's morbid, but like change and taxes, death is one of the few certainties in life. When you look at your existence through that lens, before a crisis forces you to do so, it can be extremely powerful in helping to organize your thoughts and actions in a way that nothing else can.

When we can accept it, our own mortality, or that of those closest to us, really puts things in perspective: What is it that we value? What and whom do we hold dear? What is real and meaningful for us? And when you look back on your life, how do you want to have used your time and energy while you were here? What is the mark that you want to leave on the world? How do you want people to remember you when you are gone?

Death and dying remind us that when all the external stuff falls away, what's left? You can't take that designer bag, fancy car, or impressive job title with you. It cuts to the core and brings us to the one essential thing that every human being desires—to love and be loved in return.

At the end of the day, all you have is the impact of the life you led, mostly found in close connections with others and memories you've shared. You may never know the effect you've had on strangers, and family dynamics can of course be complicated, but remember, you choose your friends, and true friends who have been a part of your journey are precious; they are there regardless of too much time having passed or petty misunderstandings.

A crisis will always give us clarity as to what's important and what we can offer one another. If you let them, what comes to the surface are love and compassion. And to be there for someone, to have the opportunity to be a healing presence in whatever form that may take, is a gift for both the giver and receiver.

As we approach this significant week in two of the world's major religions, as well as embrace the energy of Spring, think about which parts of you can bite the dust, allowing for a rebirth accompanied by a deeper commitment to honor and cherish your relationship with yourself and the healthy ones you have with others, to cultivate new connections that will enrich your journey, and to reaffirm your relationship to life itself.

Not sure what you would want to hear when you go or simply want to develop more fully whatever you can't leave behind? Learn to Walk On[5] and be able to feel good about it all, here and now.

Love Saves the Day

August 28, 2013

Darkness cannot drive out darkness; only light can do that.
Hate cannot drive out hate; only love can do that.
—Martin Luther King Jr.

When the power of love overcomes the love of power, the
world will know peace. —Jimi Hendrix (via Sri Chinmoy)

If you have read my PGGs, worked with me individually, or
come to one of my group sessions, you know that I talk a lot
about love. But the love that I talk about is not some airy-
fairy, namby-pamby, hippie-dippy notion, or one that has
been misused, watered-down or misunderstood, or something that has simply lost its meaning with lip service.

Real love is the real deal. As Mahatma Gandhi says, "Love
is the strongest force the world possesses, and yet it is the
humblest imaginable." Fifty years ago we witnessed an era
when civil rights leaders and all those who were part of that
struggle dug deep and called upon this force within themselves to withstand the immense opposition and cruelty
they experienced on a daily basis in order to transform
society as it existed at the time.

More recently we could not have had a more immediate,
direct or tangible example of this phenomenon when one
single woman, Antoinette Tuff, used it to save the lives of
more than 800 people, most of them children, from a lone,

heavily loaded, mentally ill gunman in Decatur, Georgia. If you do not know the story, or haven't seen this extraordinary woman talk about what happened, you must learn about her. (A Google search will yield numerous stories, interviews, and the entire 911 call.)

As humans we are all built from the same stuff. Love doesn't know race, sexual orientation or religion—if you are human, you can love. If you are human, you respond to love. As Antoinette Tuff and Michael Stipe say, Everybody Hurts,[6] sometimes. Everyone needs connection and affection. Compassion and empathy are palpable and are the best antidotes to fear and pain.

If you've seen me speak, you know I am always mentioning that the root of the word for courage is Latin for "heart." Which means that true bravery is about connecting to that part of yourself, knowing its innate power, and having faith in a force greater and wiser than yourself (or beyond your ego/brain).

So the next time you find yourself in a challenging situation or being attacked in some form, whether it be mental, emotional or yes, sometimes even physical, instead of using violence to counteract violence, why not call upon the most powerful weapon at your disposal: L-O-V-E.

Need a little help harnessing the heft of *your* heart? Give it a good workout, because at the end of the day, love like is a muscle—the more you use it, the stronger it will become—and who knows what miracles will occur in your life or the lives of others because of it!

HEAD VS. HEART

Girl Power

March 23, 2010

Whether man or woman, girl or boy, 15 or 50, we all have some girl power in us. We just need to take the time to discover, embrace and honor it no matter what our gender, age or sexual orientation. All it really means is adding a little bit of yin to our yang.

I was just featured on the website We Are Women Rising, where I talked about this, but due to space limitations, my first answer was edited down. It had to do with women having permission in some ways to be a little more human, to live life a bit more fully, and to explore all facets of what that means without too much judgment—whereas men might have a harder time, in many respects, exploring their feminine side regardless of their sexuality.

But I've noticed lately that a lot of women have been denying themselves certain advantages that generally come with a female form. We spend so much time and energy fitting into a "man's world" and the masculine way of operating that we forget the gifts that being "feminine" bring—and I'm not talking about being able to pose for a Victoria's Secret catalog.

As I've helped many of my clients (gals *and* guys) learn, you need to balance not only your work and life, but also your Marilyn with your Michael, and determine how to use the best of both!

Polar Shift

April 20, 2010

Massive quakes, record rainfall, perilous flooding, topsy-turvy temperatures. There is no doubt that Earth—displaying her power with last week's volcanic eruption as a kickoff to her special "Day" on April 22—is going through *something*. Whether you think of it as climate change, global warming, or that crazy concept Al Gore invented, shifts happen.

If you think of each human as his or her own self-contained world, you could say our North Pole is our mind, with its thinking/rational way of doing things, and our South Pole is the heart and gut, our more intuitive, creative MO.

We have always looked to the North Star to lead the way, but what about the Southern Sky? There would be no North without the South! One is not more important than the other. And what if the North is a little tired of doing all the heavy lifting and is starting to pass the baton to the South?

In honor of Earth Day this week, think of yourself in the process of shifting and changing, just like the planet—be aware, take care, go with the flow, and notice what happens. The Earth is crying out for ways to heal, and if you have been living a less-than-balanced life, so will you. Think of yourself as your own Mother Nature, with a super-special compass that can reset the magnetic North *and* South within you.

Under the Sea

August 24, 2010

In the movie *Ever After*, Drew Barrymore's character, Danielle, asks Leonardo da Vinci, "A bird may love a fish, signore, but where will they live?"

There are some of us who like to exist more submerged, exploring inner space and our emotions like a scuba diver or that cool deep-sea vehicle used to examine the Titanic wreckage on the ocean floor. Others fly through the air and live high above the clouds, flitting and fluttering this way and that, getting a brief overview of it all and only experiencing the external surface of the world. There are landlubbers, jet skiers and snorkelers who operate somewhere in between. Which one are you?

An adult human is about 60 percent water, so it makes sense to spend a little time in the metaphorical H_2O to get in touch with your feelings and desires, an honest assessment of what's going on within, even if it's not your regular place to hang out. The ideal is to have the best of both worlds, to be able to move between the two when the situation demands—to be either a bird that can swim or the much rarer fish that can fly (but they do indeed exist). Or maybe just change your name to Ariel.

Perhaps you're a little afraid of the abyss, don't have the right gear or you need an expert dive instructor. Or maybe you've been down there awhile and are ready to come up for some oxygen and explore new vistas; as the great Italian master assures Danielle, "Then I shall have to make you wings."

Just Go With It

While walking down the street after a bizarre week of odd "coincidences" and uncanny timings, I happened to look up and notice the announcement board of a synagogue with this quote by feminist/activist/author Robin Morgan: "Only she who attempts the absurd can achieve the impossible."

One definition of the word absurd is "inconsistent with reason, logic or common sense," which means that perhaps any decisions or actions deemed as such come from a place we can't always understand but know is somewhere deep within us.

The presidents whose holiday we just celebrated had a bit of that going on: George Washington's advisers seriously questioned his determination to cross the frozen Delaware, and he intuitively knew how to present himself as a leader for this new country. Abraham Lincoln's life is full of examples of how he went against conventional wisdom and popular opinion. Both men defied the odds by listening to their conscience, inner voice, and moral compass, and because of that, they became the great men we honor now.

Part of maturing is learning how to trust yourself despite outside influences. While advice can be helpful, when we are honest with ourselves, we are usually our own best counsel. Others may not know who we really are or have our best interests at heart. And I'm sure we can all remember times when we've dealt with the consequences of not heeding the wisdom of our gut ...

My guess is that Adam Sandler trusts his intuition about what is and isn't funny, regardless of what the Hollywood suits might say. Even in his early *SNL* days, he expressed a unique kind of silly humor that had yet to be considered commercially viable. Well, we all know how that turned out!

When I meet with clients, I am often simply validating and confirming what they already know but have been too embarrassed, in denial, doubtful or repressed to pursue or even admit. When a complete stranger is able to tell you that the "crazy" idea you have, that the thing you've always wanted to do, the life you've always dreamed of is *exactly* the direction you should be going in—based on the dots I've connected in less than two hours and without you specifically divulging what it was—then just go with it! It's the green light you've been waiting for to produce that smash box-office hit starring none other than YOU!

(Wo)Man Up

March 8, 2011

Today is the 100th anniversary of International Women's Day, so in honor of this occasion I'd like to give a special shout-out to all the men out there and encourage you to celebrate the many ways women make your lives better, acknowledge what you can learn from them, and get in touch with your feminine side with unabashed pride.

Dan Abrams just came out with a book called *Man Down*, a tome that provides extensive research proving that women are pretty much better at everything than men. Whether or not you believed that already, the key here is to remember that we are not in a Battle of the Sexes, but that everyone, regardless of the gender you are identified as or associate with, needs to demonstrate the best characteristics of both worlds.

The reality is that most men have a problem expressing emotion, long considered a "girlie" trait. The amazing irony is that as I am literally in the midst of writing this, I flip the TV channel and catch the end of Charlie Rose interviewing David Brooks about his book *The Social Animal*. Charlie, who is clearly an exception to the rule, admits how important it is for people to have the "power to express yourself and have emotional intelligence." David comments on how he struggles with this, as most men do, and how he admires Bruce Springsteen as someone who is a "manly, working-

class guy who can be emotional in a respectable way."
(Thanks fellas for validating this as I type it!)

Most men will never know What It Feels Like for a Girl,[1] so
since International Women's Day also falls on Mardi Gras
this year, what better excuse is there to "dress" in metaphorical drag and try on your womanlike alter ego for size.
I don't mean a full-on Tootsie or Ms. Doubtfire, but more
like the guys in *I Love You, Man* or The Boss in all his glory;
allow yourself to be just a little more sensitive, intuitive,
creative and expressive of what you're feeling.

Whether your birth announcement was pink or blue, we
all need to balance our Mickey with our Minnie and find a
way to make the most of *all* of who we are, without having
to shave our legs, put on a fake moustache, or become like
SNL's Pat.

A Fool's Errand

And most important, have the courage to follow your heart and intuition. They somehow already know what you truly want to become. Everything else is secondary. —Steve Jobs

Back in 2001, I visited a tech writer friend in San Francisco. He had a clunky gizmo about the size of a small hardcover book that he called an electronic jukebox; it allowed him to carry around and play his entire record collection on demand. I was blown away. Who knew that just a few years later I would own one myself, only mine was sleeker, smaller and held even more songs?

I'm a PC, but one of my most essential possessions is my iPod, and Steve Jobs' 2005 commencement speech brilliantly articulates my understanding of life and how I try to express that through my work and existence. Heeding his heart and intuition from an early age, combined with his intelligence and curiosity, allowed Steve Jobs to become the incredible innovator and visionary that he was. And because of it, I'm sure many people along the way thought he was a little cuckoo for Cocoa Puffs.

Last week the 2011 Nobel Peace Prize went to three women, including Leymah Gbowee. Featured in the film *Pray the Devil Back to Hell*, Leymah was the main force behind the courageous movement that brought Liberia back to civilization and sanity in the midst of a barbaric civil war. She listened to her heart and intuition, then strategically called upon the united and unique position of women within the culture, the power of prayer, and sheer will to transform a nation engulfed by darkness. Throughout the nonviolent campaign, she used innovative tactics that appeared crazy to many. When I watched the film, I knew I was witnessing a modern-day miracle; I was blown away.

Yesterday's holiday was named for an Italian fellow named Christopher Columbus, who in 1492 not only had the guts to assert his belief that the world was round and new lands were yet to be explored, but he actually went out and proved it. Many thought he was insane to set sail into the unknown; even his native country would not fund his so-called folly. But because he had the courage of his conviction to guide him, supported by faith and reason, he literally opened up the world for humanity to discover one other, and for better or worse, things have never been the same. When I think about what it took to make that journey, I am blown away.

We never would have survived or evolved beyond the caveman era without brave men and women like these who have stayed hungry and foolish throughout history. Because when you allow your passion and talent to be guided by a mind that receives direction from your heart, you can create something, be someone, or do something extraordinary.

Feeling a little too satiated and serious these days? Whet your appetite for life by discerning whether the direction you're going in and the ideas you have are more of a wild goose chase or the kind that will one day blow me away!

Truth No. 2
February 7, 2012

Tell me what's wrong with having a little faith in what you're feelin' in your heart.[2] —Dixie Chicks (via Patty Griffin)

I try not to think as much as possible. This serves me well for many reasons. First of all, I am somewhat dyslexic, so the more I stay out of my head, the clearer things are for me. And forget about speaking; whenever I do my seminars, what I say has to come from my heart and gut, otherwise I would get super-confused and choke from stage fright and the fear of sounding stupid.

I have learned to operate this way more and more; it reduces stress by keeping me connected to myself and in the flow of life, in harmony with who I am and what I need or want at any given moment. It is the best motivational, decision-making and communications tool I possess, because I have harnessed and developed it as such.

In the movie *Jerry Maguire*, Tom Cruise confronts Cuba Gooding Jr. about why he has not yet been offered a $10 million contract, citing that the way he is off the field is how he needs to be on the field. "You play with your head, not your heart. In your personal life? Heart. ... Play the game, play it from your heart, and you know what? I will show you the kwan. And that's the truth, man. That's the truth, can you handle it?" Jerry knew that if Rod did what he loved with love, then and only then would he be able to show him the money.

And that doesn't just hold true in the movies. Steve Tisch, a proud owner of the New York Giants, declared that the key to their big Super Bowl victory this past weekend was that they "played with more heart, more passion, and more love for each other and for the game of football."

Does that negate, replace, or even diminish all the hard work, training, strategy, talent and skill necessary to achieve such great heights? No, of course not. But it's the thing that will make the difference between a good team and a great team, a good life and a great one.

Most of us are taught to live by our heads, logic and ego, not by our hearts and guts. But only when we listen to our hearts and put love into everything are we our most authentic selves, which means living our truth. And when we are living our truth, we can more easily speak our truth and stand in our truth. And that's the best way to guarantee peace and prosperity in our lives, no matter what the circumstances.

Million-dollar contract, Lombardi Trophy or not, we are all players in the Super Bowl of Life—so are you playing with your head or your heart? Unlike Tom Cruise in his confrontation with Jack Nicholson, you can indeed handle the truth and start living in alignment with who you are and what you want to make happen both on the field and off!

COMMUNICATION
& CONNECTION

Apples & Oranges

April 28, 2010

Every day we find ourselves inundated with emails, blogs, texts, status updates, tweets galore and more. We are more connected yet disconnected than ever. So what kind of quality control do you have over you interaction with the people who matter to you most?

Technology can keep us up to date with the latest photos of your vacation or what interesting article you just read, and with even more mundane things like how bored you are at work or what you ate for breakfast. But how much of that is really filling your need to share and bond with others? Meeting with a friend for coffee or a glass of wine simply can't be replaced by a Facebook "like."

All these tools have their pros and cons when it comes to connecting with someone online versus in person. They are like apples and oranges—and I suppose it's better to have some fruit than none at all—but hopefully you have enough variety that it adds up to a tasty fruit salad.

Diana Ross sings, "Reach out and touch somebody's hand/ Make this world a better place, if you can."[1] At the end of the day, we are humans, and humans need to feel "touched" by other humans, not computers.

So make the effort to have a meaningful interaction with someone in your life on a weekly basis, and if you're not sure who that should be or "don't have the time," then consider it a sign that you need to identify which relationships would be a nutritious snack and which are just a bunch of artificial flavors.

To Tell the Truth

May 18, 2010

Actors, when interviewed about their craft, often talk about finding what the "truth" of the situation is for their part; Shakespeare tells us, "All the world's a stage, all the men and women merely players."

We are all characters in our own play or movie acting out daily scenes, but it's easy to forget that we're also the producers, writers and directors, especially when it comes to our relationships. We can, to a certain extent, cast who is in our life, assign them certain roles, and create all the drama, comedy and tragedy we want. We can even rewrite the script when we have the courage to do so.

The best way to do this is to be honest with yourself so that you can *communicate from the heart* exactly what it is you want and need. Since most people don't walk around with ESP, it's really up to you to say what you mean and mean what you say (in an appropriate way, of course!) and let the chips fall where they may, knowing that you honored what is real and true for you.

If it's not a common practice, speaking your truth can feel uncomfortable, even messy, and can make you or the other person feel like a deer in headlights—but at least you'll get to the bottom of things and set the stage to make the next scene better.

You can run but you can't hide from the truth, and telling it to yourself is the first step. Drop the curtain on being too scared or unable to see it, and shine the spotlight on what's *really* going on so you can create your starring role with a happy ending you truly deserve!

Like a Fish Needs a Bicycle

July 20, 2010

John and Abigail Adams. King Hussein and Queen Noor. Bill and Melinda Gates. Barack and Michelle Obama. Bethenny Frankel and Jason Hoppy? These are just some of the couples who appear to have a great partnership as well as romance and passion in their marriages. (The jury is still out on Bethenny and Jason ... but they looked the part for TV, didn't they?)

Back in the day (and in some parts in the world still), being hitched, especially for women, was linked to survival or a business transaction between families. In 2010, when women now lead successful, independent lives, where does that leave us with the whole question of saying "I do"? (For an interesting musing on the subject, check out Elizabeth Gilbert's recent book, *Committed*.)

The "fruits of feminism" have at times confused us all. As I recently heard in a lecture by sociologist and masculinity expert Michael Kimmel, if a woman is captain of the ice hockey team and top of her class at Yale, the guys subconsciously think, *What the heck does she need me for*?

Male of female, we all have needs, along with the things we think are needs. You may not need another person to take care of you physically, emotionally, financially and/or spiritually, but whether woman, man, or even fish,[2] everyone wants someone to love and to be loved in return. We look for partners, friends, lovers, intimacy. And that has nothing to do with what gender you are, what era you were born in, or who the object of your affection may be—it is a timeless, eternal and basic human instinct.

But before you tie the knot with another (or at any point throughout your nuptial bliss or blitz), I always recommend marrying yourself first—whatever that means to you. Because if you don't promise to love, honor and cherish yourself, why would anyone else?

Can't quite make it to the altar with yourself or your beloved? I'm no Dr. Ruth, Millionaire Matchmaker, Internet-ordained minister or justice of the peace, but by the power vested in me, I can tell you that first comes self-love, then comes some form of marriage, then comes whatever it is you desire, even if it is just a cabbage.

You've Got Mail

October 5, 2010

Although I am intrigued by the Wild West and love a good Jane Austen movie, I am always grateful that we live in a much more modern era.

One glaring difference of course, is the way we communicate. In 1860, it took mucho dinero and 10 days for the Pony Express to cross the country—a miracle feat at the time. Today, with little or no cost, we can send words, documents, letters and more for our recipients to see in mere seconds.

Women like Elizabeth Bennet spent days, weeks or even months waiting for a letter from their Darcys, and it was the only form of communication they had if they weren't in the same room. Now, the ability to have those messages delivered almost instantly can accelerate the suffering or joy that couples back then endured.

We can express ourselves and have relationships with others in myriad ways online that we never would have had the opportunity or speed to do otherwise. But as *The Social Network* writer Aaron Sorkin recently said, "Socializing on the Internet is to socializing what reality TV is to reality." So we must use the Web wisely.

Meg Ryan and Tom Hanks made it work for them, but with all the choices at our disposal, we need to have a balanced communications diet. Writing can be preferable to talking because of its clarity (when time and thought have gone into it). And putting feelings—often the most difficult to convey—on paper, in an image, or in a song can often carry more meaning. But sometimes you just need to pick up the phone.

So if you're not sure what, when, where, why or how to say what you need to say, or you want to develop more of your offline relationships rather than online "friends," take some time to discern the write stuff that truly delivers when you need it the most.

Jungle Love

October 19, 2010

The latest casualties in celebrity breakups—Courteney Cox and David Arquette, Christina Aguilera and Jordan Bratman, Ben Harper and Laura Dern, to name a few—remind us that although things may look bright and shiny on the outside, there is trouble in paradise.

Whether you have the paparazzi spotlight on you or not, this is the area of life where we are most often challenged, even if we excel at everything else. Because when it comes to relationships, it's a jungle out there. Having realistic expectations of what we want and how to go about getting it is the key to navigating that often hostile and confusing environment.

The jungle conjures up images of wild, primitive peoples, virgin (no pun intended) territories, poisonous plants, and camouflaged predators. But the reality is that it also contains myriad medicinal cures and infinite beauty and diversity—a place of healing, discovery and wonder.

Like the mighty rain forest of the Amazon, we each hold secrets and gems within us. You may first have to wield a machete to clear away the brush before you can reach a clearing and see the light of day, and see your partner in that light. It takes work—honest communication and emotional elbow grease—to get to where you are totally naked, to just *be*, without the distractions, bells and whistles or ability to hide in the denseness of all that surrounds you. That's where relationships must exist; all the rest is gravy.

If and when you reach that stripped-down place and can't embrace *yourself*, it will be much harder for your partner to do so. But if you have already uncovered and unearthed all your hidden and not-so-nice parts—and you love and accept them unconditionally while trying to improve them—then you can enter into a relationship truly whole and ready to give to another in the same way.

Whether you are traveling solo, have a plus-one, or are not quite sure what your status is on this expedition called life, know that you have the power to lead yourself out of the heart of darkness and into the bright light of day.

Moonies, Mormons & Muslims

March 29, 2011

Leadership expert Stephen Covey says, "When we listen with the intent to understand others, rather than with the intent to reply, we begin true communication and relationship building."

While sitting in Bryant Park recently, two bright young lads approached me and asked some very personal questions about my thoughts on life. Although they didn't come right out and say it, turns out they were missionaries for the Unification Church, otherwise known as the Moonies.

The funny thing is that the very day before, I had watched an interview with the creators of the highly acclaimed new musical *Book of Mormon* and the topic of missionaries and religion was top of mind, so I was more open than usual to engage with them while soaking up some sun.

Instead of automatically dismissing them, I asked where they were from (one was from Wyoming, the other from Washington state), what they had experienced since they'd been in New York, and what they hoped to gain while here. I did offer my opinion that trying to convince people of what to believe was a pretty fruitless endeavor, that individuals are on their own path and need to come to their own understanding of religion, spirituality, etc., in their own way, in their own time.

I suggested they should just do what they love and be the best version of themselves that they can be, which in itself would accomplish more than anything else. I hoped they would savor this experience of traveling and meeting so many different types of people, enriching their lives and their connection to humanity far better than actually recruiting others to their belief system.

It was a pleasant and respectful conversation, and I think we each came away feeling it was a positive interaction. I did also ask about some of the principles and the mission of the church, which I did not necessarily disagree with, as I can always find points of connection with just about anyone—because there's a little bit of all of us in each other, and a little bit of truth in everything if you listen and look for it. We have much more in common than we think we do.

With so much anti-Muslim sentiment and political divisiveness these days, on top of a crumbling planet and economy, brotherly (and sisterly!) love, under whatever label you'd like to call it, is the only glue that will hold together a planet that is currently patched together, to coin a good friend's term, with bubble gum and rubber bands.

So if you're feeling like Humpty Dumpty, Little Bo Peep's lost sheep, or Michael Stipe,[3] proselytize yourself and convert to being the biggest believer in YOU. Then get out there and make your corner of the world a little brighter for us all!

Six Seconds

September 27, 2011

I recently attended the screening of a very cool documentary called *Connected: An Autoblogography About Love, Death & Technology.* An ambitious undertaking, filmmaker Tiffany Shlain has presented some interesting ideas and factoids in a unique visual way about the history of who we are and the connections we have to each other from the past, present and where we might be headed in the future.

One of the best tidbits I learned was that if you hug someone for six seconds or more, a dose of the feel-good hormone oxytocin is released.

Many of you who have worked with me individually or in a group, or have talked to me after one of my workshops or seminars, know that I'm a big hugger. In addition to hugging my clients and audience members, I tend to hug strangers after a meaningful conversation, and even in more professional situations, say after a meeting, which may or may not be kosher, but I can't help it! I often randomly hug friends, family members and co-workers because I somehow sense they need one, and I will occasionally request one myself (especially from a super-good hugger, like my bro).

Why? I've actually never thought about it. It's just always been a natural extension of who I am, the work I do, and my love of people in general. If I had to intellectualize it, perhaps it's about sealing an interaction with a *"Yes, I see and hear you, you see and hear me, and we can show mutual love, respect and care for each other as human beings in the most tangible way."*

And let's face it, who couldn't use a hug now and then? We should be able to give and receive hugs freely, but for those of you who need to justify your request, there's a scientific explanation, because hey, who wouldn't want to get a little shot of some naturally feel-good feelings?! So forget about the economy and the Internet, because the true currency of connection is the HUG, and the good news is that it's available worldwide and is abundant in infinite amounts.

Feeling a little stressed or simply need a boost to brighten your day? Instead of reaching for that Twix bar or beer, have no fear, don't you pout, just say hello and hug it out!

Attachment Theory

December 14, 2011

We should be evolving into a new age of business with a worldview that maintains one simple proposition—that all of nature, humans, animals, earth, are interconnected and interdependent. —Anita Roddick

Throughout the past few years, it's become even more apparent that the physical glue that binds us together, whether we like it or not, is money, finance, trade. Between the crumbling of our economy and Europe's, and thus the world's, we've watched as the powers that be attempt to patch it all together with rubber bands and bubble gum in order to prevent a full-on global collapse. The technological revolution, increasing demands on natural resources, wars, extreme weather and earth changes also remind us that at this point in history we are inextricably linked and will only continue to be so.

The good news is that with the rise of social entrepreneurship and the demand for corporate social responsibility, along with the accompanying interest from newly minted and currently enrolled MBAs, even mega-companies like Wal-Mart are being pushed, whether by internal, external or a combination of both forces, to do better and be better. They are expected to make a profit *and* serve the world community at large as well as to minimize, mitigate or eradicate any negative impact of their core business. We have a long way to go, but it's a start, whether or not the intention/motivation is purely altruistic.

But that is only half the equation, as the deeper currency that holds us together is our common humanity. Because at the end of the day, we all bleed the same blood and breathe the same air, and when stripped to our core, we generally want the same things during our time on this planet: *to live a life that has purpose and meaning, and to love and be loved in return.*

So this holiday season, be a little more conscious of the way you are spending your "cash," both physically and emotionally, and reflect for a moment on the repercussions of each expenditure. What are you giving, who is that purchase affecting, and what is the receiver ultimately receiving? What kind of present can do double-duty, or last year-round or even a lifetime? Remember it really IS the thought that counts and should demonstrate love for the recipient, regardless of the price tag.

Want a gift for yourself that keeps on giving? Discovering what your *personal* gift is, and using it, will last a lifetime, and not only will you benefit, but so will your work, your family, your relationships, and the world at large!

People Who Need People

October 2, 2012

Friendship is unnecessary, like philosophy, like art, like the universe itself ... . It has no survival value; rather it is one of those things which give value to survival. —C.S. Lewis

Despite what Simon & Garfunkel once sang,[4] we are neither rocks nor islands, as many of us (especially those drawn to live in the metropolis that is New York) might want to be. The irony, of course, is that the very nature of being human means we are part of a greater whole and must interact with other human beings on many levels. Yet a sense of connection and belonging doesn't always come from the family, tribe or culture we are born into, so we must create that connection authentically, first within ourselves and then with others.

Relationships are one of the most difficult areas for us homo sapiens to navigate, and they are the biggest source of our pleasure as well as our pain. In the past three years or so, we have had an advanced course in them; I for one can say that, as difficult as it's been, I have learned some new and deeper versions of lessons I know will serve me well in the future, all of which culminated in a super-summer intensive, with this harvest season reaping the wisdom culled from that journey.

Some of those nuggets include: finding the balance between losing ourselves/being co-dependent versus isolating and becoming a monk (or a psychopath); having boundaries and not taking on/feeling responsible for another's emotional or other type of well-being; nurturing yourself, no one can know exactly what you need but you; seeing people and relationships as they really are, not how you'd like them to be. And regarding those close/intimate relationships that are more difficult or challenging, keep in mind that that person—whether parent, boss, spouse, sibling, lover, friend, child—is just the actor playing the role in a scenario you have created in order to heal and grow.

Lastly, the people you choose to allow into your life—friends, boyfriend/girlfriend, spouse/partner—should meet certain criteria. The word "friend" especially has become so diluted and watered down with the use of Facebook and social media that you need to be able to separate the wheat from the chaff and discern the **Apples and Oranges**.

The foundation of a relationship with anyone deserving of your time and energy must include understanding, appreciation and respect. You should be able to check off at least two of these to be considered a friend, and if you are fortunate to have someone in your life who truly understands, appreciates and respects you, then you are very, very lucky and should treasure and honor that relationship for the special gem that it is.

The bottom line is, You Gotta Have Friends,[5] and making time for friendships and your most important relationships is not a luxury but a necessity. It's easy to get caught up in the day-to-day busyness of life, but we need to discipline ourselves to create space for connecting with the people who love and accept us, who know and understand us, with whom we share interests and history, and with whom we have grown together, not apart.

Not sure who are your buds and who are the duds in your life? It's time to step back and determine which relationships are ripe for the pickin' and which ones have taken a lickin'!

The Magic Touch

December 3, 2013

Hello
I love myself
I love myself
I love myself
We are so happy to be alive
I love my life
Our lives are great
We love ourselves
We love being alive

"I Love My Life"
— Song and lyrics by my special friend
  Zachary Miles Lefkowitz, age 4-1/2, September 2013

When at a wake recently with my 14-year-old nephew, I recalled to him the time he was about to turn 4 and I asked if he was excited about his upcoming birthday. He began to cry hysterically, saying he didn't want to have *any* birthdays. This was because he spent a lot of time around my ailing grandmother who had just passed away in her 80s, and he made the very astute observation that getting older means you are one step closer to dying.

I asked now what it was about death that bothered him most. He did not hesitate for even a second and simply, and very seriously, said, "Because you won't have the exhilarating feeling of being alive."

I thought this was a profound answer as folks around us were suffering with the loss of our loved one; Jake homed right in on the crux of the matter: We are alive, and we should experience and treasure every moment that aliveness brings us.

Over the weekend I had my first massage in over two years, and it really brought home to me these conversations in the most basic and visceral of ways. Being alive means we are here, in a very physical body in a very physical world. Our body is our vehicle to experience all that life has to offer, so we need to love, appreciate, and take care of it—and we are also here with other human beings we are meant to love, appreciate, and take care of in a physical way.

Most of us tend to live in our heads and are quite disconnected from our bodies and/or emotions. Getting a massage—whether from a therapist or by having a friend or family member give you a little hands-on tender loving care—affirms our beingness, our aliveness, and our connection to and need for one another. Numerous studies have documented the necessity of touch, especially for newborns and the elderly; it is literally what keeps them alive and determines their health and longevity.

Diana Ross famously sang, "Reach out and touch somebody's hand / Make this world a better place, if you can."[1] If you're lucky, you have close relationships in which you can exchange physical, affectionate touch on a regular basis.

If not, there are lots of alternatives, like hugs and various forms of body work you can receive from others in appropriate ways and settings.

And sometimes the most special touch can come from a stranger, like the tourist in Bryant Park over the summer who, while having her photo taken nearby, sensed/saw me distraught and crying (even though I thought I was incognito with my sunglasses, hair covering my face and downward glance!), and in one of the most generous, kind moments I have ever experienced, gently put her reassuring, healing hand on my shoulder for a few seconds as she walked by, saying with that one gesture, *"I see you, I feel your pain; I don't know you, speak your language, or know why you are upset, but I am here to offer you what comfort I can as a fellow human being."*

So as we go down this technological highway with its isolating side effects and embark upon the holiday season with the increasingly commercial madness it brings, remember the basics: You are here, we are here, let's love our lives, love one another, and demonstrate that love and compassion in the most tangible and meaningful ways possible.

Not quite sure how? As Robin Thicke sings, don't forget that "I got it, you got it, we got the magic"[6] touch.

WOMEN'S EMPOWERMENT

I Am Woman,
Hear Me Roar!

March 9, 2010

Yesterday was International Women's Day and March is Women's History Month. As the founder of a nonprofit women's organization, The Women's Mosaic, you might have guessed what today's topic was going to be, right?

I was recently asked in an interview what it means to me to be a woman, and my response was: "As an American woman in the 21st century, it means that more than ever, I have the freedom to express myself to be who I am. I have a myriad of choices to create a life that is the most authentic and fulfilled for me, and therefore I can more readily contribute to making the world a better place for everyone."

If I were a woman in a developing country, in certain cultures, or from our recent past, then the empowerment of my life would be essential, if not the absolute key, to making my particular culture or society better. Especially in this context, living an authentic life and expressing our highest potential means that we serve as role models for the women who do not yet have the full freedoms and rights that we often take for granted, and that we honor those who came before us and sacrificed so much to get us here. We must not waste the precious opportunity we have been given.

ALL women have a mark to leave on the world—what will yours be? What kind of history will your life as a woman make? The unique gifts, talents and abilities you possess must be shared with us all!

You've Come a Long Way, Baby?

March 1, 2011

Besides coming in like a lion and going out like a lamb, March brings with it a monthlong celebration of women's history and accomplishments. This is both an exciting and confusing time for women, as we've come very far in many ways (Hillary Clinton, Justices Sotomayor and Kagan), and not so much in others (*Real Housewives*, Kardashians and the recent attack on Planned Parenthood).

In the United States, girls and young women have advanced incredibly—educationally they are doing as well as, if not better than, their male counterparts, and they make up more than half the workforce. Many women today take for granted the struggle that so many of our predecessors endured until now, and enjoy the fruits of their labor. Or do we?

Although we have had victories in terms of the legislation of equal rights and the institution of various policies and procedures in the workplace, according to the panelists at this week's "Building a Pipeline to Women's Leadership" event, the day-to-day reality is another story.

We tell our girls and young women that the sky is the limit, that they have the freedom to pursue their dreams, but women often hit a brick wall when it comes to reaching the top. With women occupying less than 15 percent of the top leadership positions across all sectors, a glass ceiling continues to exist for a variety of reasons—mostly that the women already in those positions feel threatened or companies are unsure of how inclusion will impact the bottom line, and that the demands of such jobs can't accommodate all the demands put on women as primary caregivers. A transformational culture change needs to take place.

The good news is that wall is being taken down slowly, bit by bit, old replacing new—another type, as a different PGG says, of **Changing of the Guard** initiated by women requiring more work/life balance. Now it is almost demanded from the bottom up, as millennials and great talent expect to have a certain amount of flexibility and freedom as part of the status quo, or they will look elsewhere to find it.

More and more studies are showing that as the world adapts to and honors the needs of women, everyone benefits. This approach, combined with the various types of technology now at our disposal, is truly revolutionizing the way we work, regardless of our gender.

So how do you navigate your career in the midst of such change with this precarious and unpredictable economy? We can't possibly imagine what jobs will look like in two, four or 10 years (remember just five years ago we barely had smartphones, Wi-Fi, Facebook and Twitter!). The only thing to do is get in touch with and know what it is you offer and be the best at it, continually growing and evolving into the fullest version of yourself.

I tell my clients and lecture/workshop attendees that new opportunities, situations, companies and functions are sprouting up daily, so trust that the right opening will find you or that you will recognize it when you see it. In the meantime, stay true to who you are, be the exception to every rule until it becomes the norm, and know that at the end of the day it really is about a journey, and that we will someday be able to tell our daughters *and* our sons what a long way we indeed have come.

Are You Gonna Go My Way?

July 20, 2011

No man is an island, entire of itself ... any man's death diminishes me, because I am involved in mankind, and therefore never send to know for whom the bell tolls; it tolls for thee.
—John Donne

I think there is a special place in hell for women who don't help other women. —Madeleine Albright

Whether playing in the World Cup final (or a Quidditch match), negotiating the debt ceiling, or trying for a promotion, we all rely on, communicate with, and have to work with others. Life is a team sport.

One of the reasons all those TV talent shows are so popular is that ultimately we want to see others succeed. And the voting component means we have a certain amount of power to help them; we believe in them and advocate for their victory.

Yesterday I was honored to be a facilitator at Working Mother Media's Multicultural Women's National Conference, and the one theme that resonated above all was that one woman's success should always include another's: Everyone is in a position to help someone else along the way to advance in her career and life. This takes self-awareness, understanding and each of us doing our part.

There is always satisfaction in contributing to someone else's growth—giving is always of benefit to the giver, either directly or indirectly. And hey, you never know where that person's journey will take them; it could, in fact, end up in a place where she or he (this applies to men too!) could someday advocate for you.

I created The Women's Mosaic to provide opportunities for women to connect with themselves, each other, and the world around them so that they would "recognize our unity and celebrate our diversity"—because we all are made of some version of the same stuff. I believe that social trans-formation is a result of personal transformation, so my work as a coach and motivational speaker will always encourage you to be your best self, which will then allow you, most effortlessly, to serve and work with others to create positive change in all areas of life.

Still thinking WIIFM? No matter who you are or what you do, you have to depend on others to achieve a goal, wheth-er on the soccer field, on Capitol Hill, or in the boardroom, so why not make it the most pleasant experience possible for everyone involved? Because getting from where you are to where you want to be is so much easier when you try With a Little Help From Your Friends.[1]

Rage Against the Machine

August 23, 2011

August 26 is Women's Equality Day, the anniversary of the women's vote and a day the liberation movement of the '70s declared an official holiday to recognize the full rights of women in every area of life.

Many women who were too young or not yet born at that time take for granted much of how we now exist and the choices we have, not realizing the struggles so many before us endured to get this far. We've come a long way here in America, and more recently around the globe, thanks to the dedication and sacrifice of thousands of feminists and human rights activists. But we're not there yet.

Although we've made legal advances, there is still a lot to be accomplished culturally, which is a more insidious, challenging fight. Ironically, on August 26 this year, a movie called *Colombiana* opens—the premise and marketing of which are quite deceiving, with its gorgeous star and the tagline "Revenge is Beautiful." It's the most current and blatant example of a trend in films and TV shows, written and directed by men who are glorifying extreme negative male behavior by casting the protagonist as an attractive woman.

Although they are played by women, these are not *feminine* roles, which gives us a false sense of progress.

Over the weekend, a celebrity wedding took place with much ado made about it, although I'm not sure why. Famous for being famous, these alluring, beautiful women of reality TV earn their money by selling a voyeuristic view into their lives, flaunting their extravagance and treating each other disrespectfully while most are struggling to make ends meet. They are quick to add fuel to the fantasy, fairy-tale notion of weddings without showing, at least to the world, any true understanding of the real meaning of marriage.

In NYC lately, everywhere you look women are wearing shoes that they can barely walk in; the heels, platforms and wedges keep getting higher and higher. Along with bra-burning, this was one of the things women's libbers protested against. I do love a good shoe (although I am six feet tall and would look slightly scary in four-inch platforms) and am as fond of fashion as the next gal, but not being able to walk is pushing it a bit too far—and rather literally defines the saying, being a "slave to fashion."

So yes, women are getting ahead in many ways, but when you put them in shoes that are meant for a different kind of streetwalking, they can barely move.

Men are not the enemy, and women are certainly not perfect. But we have to be careful when we see women being used as masks for the negative ways men operate or as exaggerated versions of the way men would like us to be and think we have advanced. Yes, more women than ever are in leadership positions, but that doesn't mean anything if they are just behaving with a male agenda and perspective. We need a balanced, positive dose of the best of both worlds.

Know you should be liberated but aren't quite feelin' free? Whether male or female, you may be getting duped or taken advantage of by "the man," so be sure to make the most of your positive masculine and feminine sides by asserting yourself with grace and compassion.

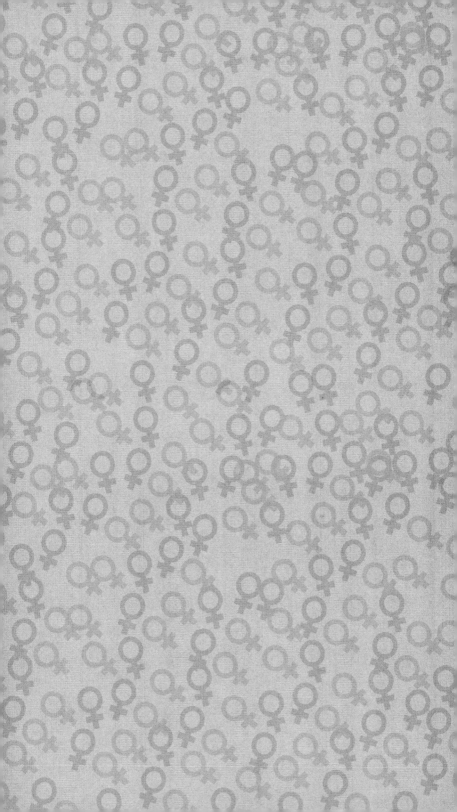

PRESENCE, PROCESS & PATIENCE

New Year's Message: Don't Believe the Hype

January 5, 2010

Happy New Year! How ya doin' with those resolutions so far? There is so much hype[i] and pressure around making huge life changes and setting goals starting January 1 that it's easy to feel utterly defeated when we don't succeed that first week, and therefore we just give up. Yes, it is the beginning of a new calendar year, so the world likes to make this time far more momentous than I believe it deserves. After an intense holiday period of excess and socialization, it is unrealistic for you to turn on a dime and start things completely fresh, especially with habits you may have had for 20 or 30 years! Change and growth do not happen overnight.

As we go through our lives, various cycles affect us and many opportunities for new beginnings occur in more authentic ways and are more in line with where we are in life at any given moment. January is a particularly good time, though, to review the past year and to THINK about and understand the changes you want to make going forward—really get reflective and go inward to see what is out of balance, what direction you want to be going in, and what small adjustments you want to make in your daily life in order to be more fulfilled. True change can happen only after you've made an internal shift, and the inner work that you do is just as valuable as the external results you desire.

Nature and the planets are more in tune with our existence and can also help guide us: new moons, full moons, and eclipses throughout the year; the Lunar New Year; the seasons (i.e., Spring and Autumnal equinoxes); our individual birthday, which is our own personal new year; and the sunrise each day are all good examples.

The important thing to remember is that life is a process. Be true to who you are and take one day at a time, knowing what is best for you and your goals. And don't beat yourself up if you don't make this first week or month the picture of perfection you envisioned on December 31. Setting a timeline and internal clock that are in harmony with YOU will be much more effective—and that will be something to celebrate at any time of the year!

Souper Douper

January 26, 2010

The old adage "patience is a virtue" is something I've been repeating to my clients a lot lately. I also tell them the story of how I made myself some delicious soup recently: I chopped up a bunch of vegetables, poured chicken stock and split peas into a big pot, and guess what? That's NOT soup ... it had to cook—gasp—for over an hour before it became anything resembling an edible meal.

Just something to keep in mind as you take on a job search or other goals and aren't getting immediate results. Don't let this world of instant email, texts and tweets throw you into a false sense of timing. As you will hear me say in nearly all of my talks, "The acorn does not become an oak tree overnight!"

So if change doesn't seem to be happening fast enough, don't stew about it. It may take some time for things to fall into place, but when it comes to achieving your goals, you want the most palatable results, not a flash in the pan ...

Snow Daze

February 16, 2010

The American way of life is all about productivity and the value we place upon it. This generally means how many hours we spent at the office, how many things we crossed off our to-do lists, projects we completed, goals accomplished.

Another way of being "productive" is by doing nothing. When used in correct proportion and at the right time, nothing can be the most productive thing we can do. That's why we should give ourselves a snow day at least once a month, regardless of the weather report!

Rest, relaxation and leisurely activities are productive because they recharge our batteries, an essential requirement that fuels us to carry on. More important, there is an ebb and flow to our lives, and when we're in a time of rest and disengagement, that's often when the big idea, the solution to the problem, the words that we've been trying to force just appear ... almost effortlessly.

You must let the ebb ebb and the flow flow. If you're too busy doing, doing, doing, thinking, thinking, thinking, then there is no room for creativity to bubble up from within or inspire from without, to discover what you really want or feel, or for you to heal.

The key is to identify *your* rhythm of ebb and flow, and how the whole work/life balance dance fills your world. Sometimes you might not realize how "off" you are ... and that's exactly what's been holding you back in your career, relationships or health.

One Day at a Time

September 14, 2010

A good friend would often quote a Yiddish saying to me: Mensch tracht, Gott lacht; Man plans, God laughs.

The renowned Buddhist monk Thich Nhat Hanh offers another perspective: "People sacrifice the present for the future. But life is possible only in the present."

In this era of instant everything and a world of answers literally at our fingertips, one of the hardest things for us to do is live in that space where we don't know what will happen next. With unemployment at record-high rates, more and more people are learning the hard way how to experience life in this manner.

People in career transition, artists, and freelancers have to operate without knowing where their next paycheck is coming from. People in new relationships are often at sea in uncharted emotional waters. Whenever we put ourselves in unfamiliar social territory or a take a trip to a place we've never been, we journey into the unknown—which is why it's so important to travel; it's one of the most natural ways to be in the present.

An easy way to add anxiety and stress in your life is to allow yourself to be overwhelmed by all the things you think you need to accomplish in the near or not-so-near future. The reality is that you can't possibly know what tomorrow will bring, so you may as well trust that the right decision or action today will lead you where you need to go, even if you don't know where you're ultimately going.

So when your life is a big question mark or an empty slate, or if you realize you're in terra incognita, find the tools you need to help you fill in the blanks, navigate your way through, or simply be present. Whether it's a lighthouse in the fog, a compass in your pocket, or taking a deep breath, trust that you will meet your authentic destination, in time and on time.

The Present of Presence

November 16, 2010

"A human mind is a wandering mind, and a wandering mind is an unhappy mind," was the conclusion of a new Harvard study whose research was conducted using an iPhone app. It is a sentiment that many religions and philosophies have proclaimed for centuries and can best be summed up by the popular phrase "Be here now."

If researchers had a window into our minds, they'd see that we are almost never fully engaged in what is right in front of us, whether we're thinking about the past or future, or simply not focused on the task at hand—and that causes unhappiness.

According to Andrew Bernstein's book *The Myth of Stress*, it's not the activity or situation that is the stressor, it's our mind's perception and reaction to the situation that causes the stress. By recognizing the reality of a circumstance and truly comprehending why it is happening, you can greatly reduce your adverse response to whatever is taking place.

I am always talking about process and "understanding where you're at." Most unpleasant situations you find yourself in are impermanent; by simply accepting that they are temporary, you can greatly increase your sense of inner peace and balance. Because life is constantly in motion, you need to learn how to "go with the flow," knowing that "this too shall pass."

Remember that if you show up mentally, as well as physically, to that meeting, event or conversation, then you've already done half the work, and the Universe can meet you halfway to create whatever it is you want or need.

Out of chaos always comes clarity. The key is learning to live happily in the unknown—keepin' it in real time—so you won't need an app to help you make sense of and make the best of any situation.

Tangible Schmangible

April 26, 2011

The true harvest of my daily life is somewhat intangible … .
It is a little star-dust caught, a segment of the rainbow which
I have clutched. —Henry David Thoreau

There is no question that there is an unseen world. The
problem is, how far is it from Midtown and how late is it
open? —Woody Allen

Ah, the paradox between poetry and practicality, art and accounting, beauty and the bottom line, meaning and metrics. Especially in the results-oriented, materially focused, high-powered metropolis that is New York, it's often challenging to communicate the value of things we are unable to touch, see or precisely measure.

I recently assigned some journaling to a client, and she seemed perplexed and not too happy about it. Her concern, she said, was that it would be difficult for her, an MIT graduate, not to have any sort of metrics or immediate tangible outcome to guide her or let her know she was doing it "correctly," which her perfectionist self needed in order to be validated in the exercise. She was not the first to be challenged by or to question the effectiveness of the solution I offered, just the first to articulate it so well!

This type of scenario has been the bane of my existence. The world of the intangible has been my field of expertise and the "meat" of my work for most of my professional life—teaching or speaking, creating programs that promote intercultural understanding and women's empowerment, individual and group coaching, even writing these little essays. Most everything I do is impactful on an internal level, enabling shifts in perception and healing to take place, so my challenge has always been in how to grade, evaluate, measure or assure the merit of such things: How do you quantify understanding, inspiration, identity and transformation?

With flowers and trees now blooming all around us, remember that they didn't just magically appear overnight, as unseen forces were at work during the barren winter months. The result is tangible, but the process itself is something too. Fertile soil, sunshine, water, time and Nature's mysterious special sauce work consistently in harmony behind the scenes, making it come together for us to once again enjoy the gorgeous potpourri of colors and shapes.

Feeling like your Spring needs to be sprung? You might just need a little tending to your garden, fertilizing it with a big dose of process, presence and patience in order to bring on the blossom and have Everything Coming Up Roses[2] for you again!

Here Today, Gone Tomorrow

May 24, 2011

Well, we're still here. And although the Apocalypse did not occur on May 21, we are experiencing a type of end of days—or at least era—with *The Oprah Show* shutting down after 25 years! How am I going to exercise my tear glands and release oxytocin on a regular basis now??

Fanatic follower or not, you can't deny that Oprah Winfrey has used her platform for educational and inspirational purposes with class and dignity, affecting millions all over the world in a positive way; she's been an oasis in a TV landscape filled with Jerry Springers, Jersey/Atlanta/NYC/Mob *Wives*, and a million *CSIs* and *Law & Orders*.

One of Oprah's "mandates" is to live your best life. The great thing about the end of days prophecy was that, although a joke to many, it perhaps for a minute forced us think about what we would like to do before our final day arrives, whether by mass destruction or natural causes. Acknowledging the inevitability of death can be a powerful motivator, and if you've ever heard me speak, you know my mantra is "Your time and energy are your most precious resources." So the question is: What are you doing with the breath, pulse and intelligence you possess while you still have it?

Another thing Oprah always talks about is the universal wisdom of being present, of living in the moment. Most people can spend days, months and years regurgitating the past or worrying about the future, which is one of the biggest wastes of that precious time and energy.

It's a delicate dance that requires deep discipline and profound love of life to "live each day as if it were your last" and to know that "there's no time like the present." What will always snap us back to these truisms, at least temporarily, is the instant devastation we observe or experience like the recent tornadoes, volcanoes and earthquakes, violent acts, or even simple accidents—recognizing that our physical belongings at the least, and our physical bodies at the worst, can be wiped out literally in a heartbeat.

The good news and reality is more likely that we are indeed coming to the End of the World As We Know It[3]—and perhaps that's not such a bad thing, you might even feel fine ... But if you're sensing a little doom in your days, find more practical ways to uplift your spirit and keep you here on the planet so you can make the most of who you are every minute of every day!

A More Perfect Union

June 28, 2011

One of my favorite movies, *Bottle Shock*, is about the then-nascent California wine industry and its victory over the French in a blind taste test held in celebration of the 1976 bicentennial. The film is based on the true story of a man who ditched his legal career to pursue a dream of making the best wine possible. Jim Barrett put his life into Chateau Montelena; to do so was a huge risk, and he had to have unwavering faith in himself and trust in the process of such a delicate, complex and time-consuming task, whose results were not necessarily guaranteed.

As with any such journey, there were many twists and turns and ups and downs along the way, but in the end he triumphed not only because he beat the French at their proudest export, but also because in doing so, he blew the field wide open for quality wine to be produced in countries around the globe, and the world has never been the same.

Orson Welles, in his famous commercials, would say, "We will sell no wine before its time." It takes time for lasting success to develop, and there is no better activity than viticulture to demonstrate that. There are cycles of planting, pruning, harvesting, fermenting and numerous other magical, alchemical things that need to happen for that perfect glass to arrive at your table. As I always say in my seminars,

"Remember that grapes do not turn into wine overnight!"

With last week's Solstice officially ushering in the summer, we are reminded that "to everything there Is a season."[4] The historic vote to legalize same-sex marriage in New York three days later was decades in the making; several societal changes and generations of progress had to occur in order to have the majority of the population now be "ripe" for its acceptance, and we are all stronger and better for having gone through the process.

Since we are halfway through the year, be sure you are working internally and externally toward whatever goals you set for yourself; know that as long as you consistently do things that you love and care about, you are fertilizing your life, making it as rich as possible. Focus your thoughts, words and deeds in the direction you want to be going, knowing that all will come to fruition with a perfect union of patience, persistence and perseverance—in time and on time.

You can't put the cart before the horse, so if you're feeling a little frustrated and impatient in pursuit of your passions, don't pop your cork. Breathe, and like a good sommelier, learn how to tell others about the uniqueness and quality of *your* vintage so you can make your dream a reality!

The Patience of Patients

September 11, 2012

Patience is not passive; on the contrary, it is active; it is concentrated strength. —Edward G. Bulwer-Lytton

Patience is bitter, but its fruit is sweet.
—Jean-Jacques Rousseau

I find it curious that the word *patient* has two distinct meanings, yet both encompass bearing some level of discomfort over a period of time (even if it's just being in the waiting room of a doctor's office!).

We all have individual and collective anniversaries, memories and milestones that we share to some degree or another; regardless if they were positive or negative, hopefully we are able to see the growth and healing that has since transpired. Tomorrow will mark three months since my mom underwent open-heart surgery (see **Heart & Soul**), and after minute-by-minute, hour-by-hour, day-by-day and week-by-week attention, care and rest, she was back out at her clubs (yes, plural and yes, as in nightclubs/dancing) this past weekend.

It's truly amazing what time can do when you give it a chance to work its magic. But in this action-oriented, left-brained, results-demanding, pill-for-everything, instant-information, fast-food society, time gets a bad rap. Faster is perceived to always be better, and action trumps rest in the eyes of others. With almost everything available to us on demand and with bottles of 5-hour Energy at our disposal, we've grown impatient beyond reasonable expectations.

"Patience is a virtue" and "Time heals all wounds" are two of my favorite adages because they express the type of "muscles" I've exercised and "tools" I've developed—you guessed it, over time—as they become realities when you see the proof in the pudding. In my coaching and speaking work, I am constantly trying to get folks to understand that although we are living in a 24/7, instant-access technological wonderland, Nature does not work that way—the acorn does not become an oak tree overnight!

Clients are often frustrated with me when I advise them not to do anything that they consider "doing" or that will have a direct and immediate impact on their job search or life's path. What I suggest doesn't mean they should sit around twiddling their thumbs; it's about understanding that there is a process, and it's inner work through activities that don't seem "productive" or results-producing, when in fact they are the true heavy lifting of personal growth. We all have wounds that need to be healed, and not addressing them or allowing them the time and space to do so is often what blocks us from moving forward; therefore, that is where time and energy need to be spent!

I am always planting seeds when I work with clients, giving them ideas and suggestions they may not necessarily be ready to implement immediately but should think about, pay attention to, and consider down the road. I also guide them toward the many stepping-stones they need to take on the path to their ultimate goal, whether or not they are aware of that goal.

The philosopher Kierkegaard said, "Patience is necessary, and one cannot reap immediately where one has sown." I have had the pleasure of finding out recently how many of my clients are beginning to reap what they have sown, with projects, jobs and opportunities that are only now coming to fruition, one, two and even four years after we met, which is extremely rewarding and only reinforces the "method to my madness."

The paradox and balancing trick, of course, is that time doesn't stop; it can pass us by quickly, so we need to be in motion with it and "make hay while the sun shines." On the other hand, we need to accept and be comfortable with what is realistic in terms of how long things take to change and develop. Just as we are all students in this school called Life, we are all patients in the healing of our lives, which is part of what growing means—healing the wounds of our past so we can move forward ever more healthy and strong.

Need a little help on your journey from acorn to oak tree, or from wounded to well? Take a look to see how you can use the gift of time to speed things up or slow them down, keeping in mind that this might just be the opposite of what you think ...

The Rhythm of the Saints

April 30, 2013

There is a tree outside my window that marks the passage
of time, with its cycle of leaves that float to the ground in
Autumn, its branches that remain bare through the Winter
until one day I wake up to find they have sprouted buds—
which eventually become the lush greenery of Summer
before they slowly turn yellow, fall off, and go dormant
again until Spring. No matter how extreme the weather—and
we've had some doozies lately—my little tree never ceases to
amaze me with its remarkable and reliable transformation
year in and year out.

Those of us who were born or became city slickers find
ourselves existing in a concrete jungle filled with technological wonder and have to make a conscious effort to get
our green on. But spending time in Nature is not just about
breathing fresh air and taking a hike in the forest or a swim
at the beach; it's about realigning ourselves with how the
world really works, not how us humans have manipulated it
or want it to be.

It's easy to forget that we are made up of the same elements
as the trees, birds, oceans and stars, and that we have
within us an innate nature that, if we tune into it, will always
serve us exactly as it should. But this means we must tune
out the loud voices and headlines screaming for our attention, telling us how we should feel, what we should do,

whom we should fear, or what we should buy; we need to block out the many warped perceptions of how long things should take and in what way they should transpire.

Spending quality time with yourself each day strengthens your "you muscle" so you can get to know, love and accept who you are and operate accordingly. Music is a powerful tool to counteract the "noise" of the day and to get you into your own space, so make sure you are feeding your soul with a good dose of melodies, harmonies and/or lyrics that uplift, soothe or energize depending on what you need at that moment to create peace in your little world.

What if you don't quite fit in the status quo? For example, being an introvert and a night owl living in a society that favors and rewards extroverts and early birds might require more of an effort to go against the grain, but the more you go with your own flow and march to the beat of your own drum, the less stressed and more rewarding life will be.

You can then experience the joy of synchronicity, because it is when you are so connected to yourself and the Universe that "magic" happens: You see a scene, hear a line in a movie, or come across a book that speaks directly to you; you find out about an event or run into a person who helps you get your dream job; or perhaps you receive an unexpected check in precisely the amount you needed just in the nick of time. It all comes down to having trust and faith in yourself and your path—and trusting that the very process of life is the best way to honor being alive.

Those of you who know me know that one of my favorite sayings is that everything happens "in time and on time." In Eastern philosophy, this goes hand in hand with the concept of *wu wei*, loosely translated as "non-action" or "effortless doing." I am also here to remind you to have patience, because life doesn't happen overnight or like an instant message; there is ebb and flow, a shedding and a blossoming, and an unfoldment that is under the control of something far wiser than our little pea brains.

Feeling a bit tone-deaf trying to find your own rhythm in a world of distraction and dissonance? Think of yourself as a piano teacher with a fancy metronome and get yourself back in the groove to make beautiful music in every area of your life!

It Takes Two to Tango

November 12, 2013

I always like to remind folks who attend my talks that we are living in *extraordinary* times. Now more than ever we need to listen to our hearts and march to the beat of our own drum. Yet we are not solo performers on this stage—more like duets, with the Universe as our partner—in what I like to think of life as the dance of life. There is ebb and flow, push and pull, reap and sow.

In our technologically advanced, left-brain-evolved world, we think we can do more and know all the answers in making things happen for ourselves. But the truth is that we are only half the equation; the Universe, with its great unknown and unseen power, process and nature, is the other half.

There is a sublime order to things in our world if we only allow ourselves to honor it, regardless of how long our journey takes or what form or shape the fruit of it bears—and the Universe always knows better than our little pea brains. There is a method to its seeming madness and oft-lengthy timeline, but the more we resist its infinite wisdom, the more we suffer, the more mess is made, the more there is to clean up, and the longer it can take to get back on track.

Instead, we must learn to go with the flow—not in a loosey-goosey kind of way, but with faith and confidence, like a farmer planting his seeds, knowing that the sun will rise tomorrow and that what goes up must come down.

Any artist, dancer, musician or athlete understands that practice and technique will get you only so far; at some point you have to let go and allow the Universe to do its thing. In other words, no matter what you are working toward—getting a new job, growing a business, reaching health goals, or improving relationships—you need to simply "do your best and surrender the rest."

If you haven't seen the external results you desire, take a moment to slow down and reflect. If you've been paying attention, you'll notice you've been undergoing some major inner reconstructing and rearranging of molecules, experiencing a deep emotional and mental detox encouraging you to let go of the past in order to move forward; this too is part of the dance. Sound familiar? If not, and you've been feeling blocked at every turn, ignoring the call to do this type of internal work is probably to blame—and it is easy to correct.

The beauty of dancing with the big U is that once you get in sync with it, things actually get in sync with you, and stuff starts to happen, as I always say, "in time and on time"—and often more miraculously than you could have ever imagined.

Not sure of what steps to take next or feeling like you wanna rock right now? It Takes Two[5] to make a thing go right, so let a special someone, perhaps even me, help you make it outta sight!

MIXTAPE COLLECTION

Looking for some inspiration regarding your ideal career and life's purpose? Here's Mixtape #1:

A Tale of Two Streets
All That You Can't Leave Behind
At Your Service
Freeze-Frame
Labor Pains
Life Class
Money Makes the World Go Round
Tangible Schmangible
The Price Is Right?
They Might Be Giants
Work It
You Say You Want a Revolution

Looking from some inspiration because you're feeling blocked or need to make a change? Here's Mixtape #2:

Beauty in the Breakdown
Drop It Like It's Hot
Get Up, Stand Up
New Rules
Roots
Shake Your Groove Thing
The Experiment
The Heat Is On/Under Pressure
The Year of Living Uncomfortably
Validation Nation

Looking for some inspiration to relax and digitally detox? Here's Mixtape #3:

A Body at Rest
Chillax
Slow Down, You Move Too Fast
Summatime
The Pleasure Principle
Tiptoe Through the Tulips

Looking for some inspiration after experiencing loss? Here's Mixtape #4:

All That You Can't Leave Behind
Joni Mitchell Never Lies
The Magic Touch

Looking for some inspiration going through/while in a relationship? Here's Mixtape #5:

Jungle Love
Like a Fish Needs a Bicycle
One Is the Magic Number
People Who Need People
To Tell The Truth
Under the Sea

Need to get through the holidays?
Here's Mixtape #6:

High Anxiety
New Year Don't Believe the Hype
Sing Out Loud
Thank the Turkeys Too!
Whoa, Nelly

Looking for some inspiration from/wanna learn more about Kristina's journey? Well, duh, they're ALL about my journey (we write what we need to read and teach what we need to learn!), but here are some more biographical ones in Mixtape #7:

A Body at Rest
All Roads: Same Place
Drop It Like It's Hot
Happy
Life Class
Life Is Like a Box of Chocolates
Minute to Win It
New Rules
Own It
The Magic Touch
Vision Quest

Create your own mixtape(s) here:

_____

_____

_____

_____

_____

_____

_____

I would love to know which PGG combinations helped you through a particular situation. Share your thoughts or comments about these mixtapes or post your own on the Personal Growth Gab Facebook page.

PGG PLAYLISTS: VOLUME ONE

A list of all the tunes referenced in the book—why not make a cool playlist to get you groovin' to your growth!

SELF-EXPRESSION

1. "Freedom! '90," George Michael.
2. "Born This Way," Lady Gaga.
3. "Express Yourself," Madonna.
4. "Butterfly," Corinne Bailey Rae.
5. "Show Me What You Got," Jay-Z.
6. "Heigh-Ho," The Dwarfs (from the animated *Snow White and the Seven Dwarfs*).
7. "Tumblin' Down," Ziggy Marley and the Melody Makers.
8. "Moves Like Jagger," Maroon 5, featuring Christina Aguilera.
9. "Sing," The Muppets and friends.
10. "Do-Re-Mi," Julie Andrews et al (as Maria and the von Trapp children in *The Sound of Music*).
11. "Dream On," Aerosmith.
12. "Shake Your Groove Thing," Peaches & Herb.
13. "You Should Be Dancing," Bee Gees.

THE JOURNEY

"Steppin' Out," Joe Jackson.
1. "Amazing Grace," Traditional hymn (by John Newton).
2. "Material Girl," Madonna.
3. "Lady Marmalade," Christina Aguilera, Lil' Kim, Mya and Pink.
4. "Roxanne," The Police.
5. "Just a Gigolo," David Lee Roth.
6. "Another Brick in the Wall," Pink Floyd.
7. "The Miseducation of Lauryn Hill," Lauryn Hill.
8. "Emmylou," First Aid Kit.
9. "#Selfie," The Chainsmokers.

SELF-LOVE & CARE

"Tiptoe Through the Tulips," Tiny Tim.
"High Anxiety," Mel Brooks.
1. "Zip-a-dee-doo-dah," James Baskett (as Uncle Remus in *Song of the South*).
2. "The Pleasure Principle," Janet Jackson.
3. "Hot Fun in the Summertime," Sly and the Family Stone.
4. "One Is the Loneliest Number," Three Dog Night.
5. "One," U2.
6. "One in a Million You," Larry Graham.
7. "Numero Uno," Starlight.
8. "One Love," Bob Marley & the Wailers.
9. "Always on the Run," Lenny Kravitz.

CHALLENGING TIMES

"The Heat Is On," Glenn Frey.
"The Roof Is on Fire," Grandmaster Flash.
1. "Message in a Bottle," The Police.
2. "Control," Janet Jackson.
3. "Under Pressure," Queen and David Bowie.
4. "Light My Fire," The Doors.
5. "Burning Down the House," Talking Heads.
6. "Put a Little Love in Your Heart," Dolly Parton.
7. "Got 'Til It's Gone," Janet Jackson, featuring Q-Tip and Joni Mitchell.
8. "Things Can Only Get Better," Howard Jones.
9. "Kumbaya," Traditional folk song.
10. "Let Go," Frou Frou.
11. "Stronger (What Doesn't Kill You)," Kelly Clarkson; "Stronger," Kanye West.

SELF-REFLECTION

"Holiday Road," Lindsey Buckingham.

"Drop It Like It's Hot," Snoop Dogg, featuring Pharrell.

1. "The 59th Street Bridge Song (Feelin' Groovy)," Simon & Garfunkel.
2. "Summertime," DJ Jazzy Jeff & The Fresh Prince.
3. "Ghostbusters," Ray Parker Jr.
4. "Life in One Day," Howard Jones.
5. "Things Can Only Get Better," Howard Jones.
6. "Freeze-Frame," The J. Geils Band.
7. "Ebony and Ivory," Paul McCartney and Stevie Wonder.
8. "Slip Slidin' Away," Paul Simon.
9. "Thank U," Alanis Morissette.
10. "Heart and Soul," Hoagy Carmichael.
11. "Time of the Season," The Zombies.
12. "Digging in the Dirt," Peter Gabriel.
13. "Happy," Pharrell Williams.

CHANGE & TRANSITION

"Aquarius/Let the Sunshine In," Fifth Dimension.

1. "Time to Change," The Brady Bunch.
2. "Use the Force," Jamiroquai.
3. "Don't Worry, Be Happy," Bobby McFerrin.
4. "Changes," David Bowie.
5. "Fly Like an Eagle," Steve Miller Band.
6. "Three Little Birds," Bob Marley & the Wailers.
7. "Don't You Worry 'Bout a Thing," Stevie Wonder.
8. "Lean On Me," Bill Withers.
9. "Right Here, Right Now," Jesus Jones.
10. "Anthem," Leonard Cohen.
11. "Ch-Check It Out," Beastie Boys.
12. "Hot Stuff," Donna Summer.
13. "Stayin' Alive," Bee Gees.
14. "A Change Is Gonna Come," Sam Cooke.
15. "A Spoonful of Sugar," Julie Andrews (as Mary Poppins in
    Mary Poppins).

CURRENT EVENTS & GLOBAL PERSPECTIVE

"Mercy Mercy Me (The Ecology)," Marvin Gaye.
"Get Up, Stand Up," Bob Marley & the Wailers.
1. "What's Going On," Marvin Gaye.
2. "Let's Get It On," Marvin Gaye.
3. "Revolution," The Beatles.
4. "You Can't Always Get What You Want," Rolling Stones.
5. "Bridge Over Troubled Water," Simon & Garfunkel.
6. "Let There Be Peace on Earth," Folk song.
7. "No More Trouble," Bob Marley & the Wailers.
8. "Rock the Casbah," The Clash.
9. "All You Need Is Love," The Beatles.
10. "Love the One You're With," Crosby Stills and Nash.
11. "It Ain't Over 'Til It's Over," Lenny Kravitz.
12. "What the World Needs Now Is Love," Burt Bachrach.
13. "On a Clear Day (You Can See Forever)," Barbra Streisand.
14. "Higher Ground," Stevie Wonder.
15. "Peace Train," Cat Stevens.
16. "Power to the People," John Lennon.
17. "Shaking the Tree," Peter Gabriel.
18. "Strength, Courage and Wisdom," India.Arie.
19. "Use the Force," Jamiroquai.
20. "Imagine," John Lennon.
21. "Joy and Pain," Rob Base and DJ E-Z Rock.

LOVE

1. "Let Love Rule," Lenny Kravitz.
2. "Where Is the Love?" The Black Eyed Peas.
3. "Revolution," The Beatles.
4. "Free to Be ... You and Me," The New Seekers.
5. "Walk On," U2.
6. "Everybody Hurts," R.E.M.

HEAD VS. HEART

"Under the Sea," Samuel E. Wright (as Sebastian in *The Little Mermaid*).
1. "What It Feels Like for a Girl," Madonna.
2. "Truth No. 2," Dixie Chicks.

COMMUNICATION & CONNECTION

"Jungle Love," Morris Day and the Time.
"People," Barbra Streisand.
1. "Reach Out and Touch (Somebody's Hand)," Diana Ross.
2. "Tryin' to Throw Your Arms Around the World," U2.
3. "Losing My Religion," R.E.M.
4. "I Am a Rock," Simon & Garfunkel.
5. "Friends," Bette Midler.
6. "Magic," Robin Thicke.

WOMEN'S EMPOWERMENT

"I Am Woman," Helen Reddy.
"Are You Gonna Go My Way," Lenny Kravitz.
1. "With a Little Help From My Friends," The Beatles (or Joe Cocker—like 'em both!)

PRESENCE, PROCESS & PATIENCE

"The Rhythm of the Saints," Paul Simon.
1. "Don't Believe the Hype," Public Enemy.
2. "Everything's Coming Up Roses," Rosalind Russell (as Rose Hovick in *Gypsy*).
3. "It's the End of the World As We Know It (and I Feel Fine)," R.E.M.
4. "Turn! Turn! Turn!" The Byrds.
5. "It Takes Two," Rob Base and DJ E-Z Rock.

CUSTOM PLAYLISTS:

PGG AT THE MOVIES

A Few Good Men (1992)
Back the the Future (1985)
Beauty and the Beast (1991)
Becoming Chaz (2011)
Be Kind Rewind (2008)
Born Yesterday (1950)
Bottle Shock (2008)
Cinderella (1950)
Clash of the Titans (2010)
Colombiana (2011)
Connected: An Autoblogography About Love, Death & Technology (2011)
Django Unchained (2012)
Eat Pray Love (2010)
Eternal Sunshine of the Spotless Mind (2004)
Ever After: A Cinderella Story (1998)
Forrest Gump (1994)
Four Weddings and a Funeral (1994)
Frankenstein (1931)
Freaky Friday (2003)
Ghostbusters (1984)
Going the Distance (2010)
Groundhog Day (1993)
Grown Ups (2010)
High Anxiety (1977)
Hitch (2005)
I Love You, Man (2009)
I'm the One That I Want (2000)
Jerry Maguire (1996)
Just Go With It (2011)
Justin Bieber: Never Say Never (2011)

Lincoln (2012)
Man on a Mission (2010)
Mommie Dearest (1981)
Moonstruck (1987)
Mrs. Doubtfire (1993)
National Lampoon's Vacation (1983)
Pray the Devil Back to Hell (2008)
Pride and Prejudice (2005)
Reality Bites (1994)
Remember the Titans (2000)
Roots (1977)
Scream (1996)
17 Again (2009)
Silver Linings Playbook (2012)
Snow White and the Seven Dwarfs (1937)
Something's Gotta Give (2003)
Star Wars (1977)
Strictly Ballroom (1992)
The Blind Side (2009)
The Change-Up (2011)
The Devil Wears Prada (2006)
The Horse Whisperer (1998)
The Little Mermaid (1989)
The Lord of the Rings (trilogy)
The Sessions (2012)
The Social Network (2010)
The Wizard of Oz (1939)
Tootsie (1982)
Vision Quest (1985)
When a Stranger Calls (2006)
You, Me and Dupree (2006)
You've Got Mail (1998)

AHA MOMENTS:

NOTES:

TO-DO LIST:

NOTES:

INDEX

A

A Body at Rest 99
A Fool's Errand 254
A More Perfect Union 313
A Tale of Two Streets 198
All Roads: Same Place 210
All That You Can't
  Leave Behind 238
American Horror Story 200
An Apple for the Teacher 60
And S/He Was 24
Apples & Oranges 261
Are You Gonna Go My Way? 292
At Your Service 16
Attachment Theory 275
Attitude of Gratitude 128

B

Battle of the Bulge 194
Be Kind Rewind 153
Beauty & the Beast 220
Beauty in the Breakdown 123
Blast from the Past 146

C

Changing of the Guard 173
Chillax 93
Conjunction Junction 149

D

Déjà Vu All Over Again 190
Discipline Is Not a Dirty Word 81
Don't Tread on Me 10
Don't Worry, Be Happy 177
Drop It Like It's Hot 161

E

Election 40

F

Fear Factor 118
Follow the Leader 196
For Weddings and a Funeral 192
Free Love 233
Freedom Is Fashionable 20
Freeze-Frame 147

G

Get Up, Stand Up 207
Girl Power 247
Going the Distance 56
Groundhog Day, the Grammys
  & Gaga 47
Grown-Ups 224

H

Happy 163
Heart & Soul 155
Here Today, Gone Tomorrow 311
High Anxiety 89
Holiday Road 142

I

I Am Woman, Hear Me Roar 287
Into the Woods 140
It Takes Two to Tango 321

J

Joni Mitchell Never Lies 121
Jungle Love 269
Just Desserts 235
Just Go With It 250

L

Labor Pains 14
Leap of Faith 54
Let Love Rule 231
Let the Sun Shine In 181
Life Class 73
Life Is Like a Box of
 Chocolates 65
Lighten Up 91
Like a Fish Needs a Bicycle 265
Lost? 51
Love Saves the Day 241
Lucky Charms 4

M

Mercy Mercy Me 189
Minute to Win It 18
Mommie Dearest 102
Money Makes the World
 Go Round 49
Moonies, Mormons & Muslims 271

N

New Rules 28
New Year's Message: Don't Believe
 the Hype 301

O

Of Pride & Prejudice 5
One Day at a Time 305
One Is the Magic Number 95
Out of Control 112
Out With the Old,
 In With the New 169
Own It 39

P

Peas on Earth 202
People Who Need People 277
Polar Shift 248
Preparing for Liftoff 137

R

Rage Against the Machine 294
Reality Bites 183
Roots 97

S

Sending Out an SOS 107
Service & Self 3
Shake Your Groove Thing 36
Sing Out Loud 31
Six Seconds 273
Slow Down,
 You Move Too Fast 136
Smile in Your Liver 85
Snow Daze 304
Something's Gotta Give 175
Souper Douper 303
Steppin' Out 52
Summatime 139

T

Tangible Schmangible 309
Thank the Turkeys Too! 108
The Blind Side 151
The Change-Up 179
The Experiment 33
The Heat Is On/Under Pressure 114
The Magic Touch 280
The Passion of Passover 135
The Patience of Patients 315
The Pleasure Principle 87
The Present of Presence 307
The Price Is Right? 58
The Rhythm of the Saints 318
The Roof Is On Fire 116
The Year of Living Uncomfortably 171
They Might Be Giants 217
Tiptoe Through the Tulips 83
To Tell the Truth 263
Truth No. 2 256

U

Under the Sea 249
USA 8

V

V 22
Validation Nation 158
Vision Quest 70

W

What's Your Number? 63
Wherever You Go,
   There You Are 144
Whoa, Nelly 68
(Wo)Man Up 252
Work It 26
World Wide Web 204
Write or Die 12

Y

You Are Not Alone 110
You, Me & Dupree 125
You Say You Want a
   Revolution 214
Your Epidermis Is Showing 6
You've Come a
   Long Way, Baby? 289
You've Got Mail 267

ACKNOWLEDGMENTS

It is perhaps an overused analogy to talk about giving birth to a project, but as I write this just before going to publication, I realize that it was exactly nine months ago that I first met with my editor Elise Goldberg and designer Christina Quintero.

Now, of course that was not the first time I *met* them. Ten years ago Christina was a fresh-faced recent college grad when she approached TWM's table at an NYU job fair, and I instantly hired her as an intern to create our very first printed newsletter (and subsequently two more)—so she knew my crazies and style, and lo and behold, lucky for me she ended up having a career at, and is now a senior art director for, a major publishing house!

And then there is Elise Goldberg, who came to see me speak at the New York Public Library sometime in 2010, signed up to be on my mailing list, then inadvertently unsubscribed herself, which I discovered when out of the blue I got an email from her asking why she hadn't been receiving the weekly emails she'd been enjoying so much. Little did she know that query would mean four years later she'd be living and breathing 131 of them for several months, because after working with her and finding out she was a former copy editor at *The New York Times* ...

In thinking about who would help me bring this baby to life, true to form in how everything in my life weaves together, these two—I dubbed them my Dream Team—were my first choices, and both agreed to do it. Thank you, Universe! They have exceeded even my best expectations for working together, and how great is it that we are all night owls (seriously, you have no idea how that helped!)?!? Elise could not have been more committed, diligent and thorough, fact-checking and copyediting and thinking for me on those plug paragraphs; she simplified the process and had the patience and humor to go over it all with me! She said she had a hard time editing the words "my amazing editor Elise"—well get used to it, because I hope to do many more projects with you! Christina is cool as a cucumber and somehow reads my mind, understands my clunky language, and translates effortlessly what I want to convey on the page while providing technical expertise and professional opinions along the way. She truly amazes me with her ability to do 10 million projects at once with such finesse! Both of you are incredibly talented and were such a pleasure and so easy to work with. I am eternally grateful for all the time, effort and energy you put into *PGG*, especially when I started having "labor pains" and put our production schedule into high gear. You met me every step of the way, and I view this book as a true collaboration. Thank you for making this dream become a reality!

In addition to my Dream Team, my sincere thanks go to Monica Chelchowski Hens, Heather Floyd and Kekla Magoon, who provided significant feedback and input into the pre- and post-drafts. I want to especially thank Monica, who was *PGG*'s first cheerleader and signed on to edit this project in 2011, when I first decided to do a book. Although she didn't end up editing the final version (three and a half years later!), we did keep her original foreword—because it was just that perfect.

I also want to thank Monica, Diane DiResta, Victor Fidel, and my brother David Leonardi, who affirmed my talent as a writer and the value of the PGGs; Matthew Lore who offered me industry advice and connections; and Melissa Estévez—she attended one of my earliest corporate seminars and quickly proclaimed herself my first fan, and was the first to ask me (and then hound me) about when I was going to publish a book. Aquí está! And to a few special clients: Linda, Sheree and Nazneen for putting your trust in me over the long haul and making me a better coach and human being, which has influenced my writing greatly.

And like all of you, I am in the midst of my own personal growth and have received much assistance along the way! I am so grateful to all those who have helped me evolve and supported me on my journey thus far with love, healing, encouragement, food, finances, supplies, expertise, wisdom and laughter—I would not be who and where I am without you: Michele, Sharón, Noga, Lilith, Kekla, Heather, Maryanne, Scott, Kevin, Alex, Josh, Kerry, Andrew, Alan, Padma, Melanie, Paige, Ronni, Sally, Blaise, Juanita, Chris, Mara, David, Kathryn, and to my dear friend Danielito, whose talent and brilliance I deeply admired, and who shocked and honored me many years ago by telling me that I was a really good writer, but I didnt believe him. Well, I guess I have a bit more confidence these days ...

ABOUT THE AUTHOR

Kristina Leonardi is a motivational speaker, facilitator, career/life coach and author, who provides a framework for individuals to make the most of their personal and professional lives, allowing them to recognize, connect to and fulfill their role in the world at large. A compelling, "inspiring" and "down-to-earth" lecturer with unique yet practical perspectives on the topics of career development, work/life wellness and personal growth, she is in high demand as a speaker and has presented to groups of professionals at Saatchi & Saatchi, UBS, Ogilvy & Mather, New York's Science, Industry and Business Library, the American Women's Business Association, Junior League, and Human Resources Association of New York.

Kristina is also an executive coach and consultant in the areas of employee engagement and leadership development for small businesses, start-ups and corporations. She offers individual and group coaching privately as well as in affiliation with New York Women in Communications, and previously with Women for Hire, Craigslist Foundation Nonprofit Bootcamp and Step Up Women's Network.

In 2001, she founded The Women's Mosaic (TWM), a nonprofit organization that produced more than 100 diverse, dynamic events in its first 10 years, bringing together more than 5,000 women of all backgrounds to connect to themselves, each other, and the world around them.

Kristina holds a B.A. in International Relations from Boston University and has taught for more than 15 years at New York University's School of Continuing and Professional Studies, in both the Tisch Center for Hospitality, Tourism and Sports Management, and the department of Career, Education and Life Planning. She was listed as one of *Hispanic* magazine's Top Latinas of 2004, received Tango Diva's 2007 Diva Visionary Award, was honored by the WNBA's New York Liberty as part of their 2009 Inspiring Women Night, and has been featured in Forbes.com, Inc.com, *Psychology Today* and *The Huffington Post*.

Since launching *Personal Growth Gab* (PGG) in January 2010, Kristina has formed an avid and faithful following ("they really help me"; "I save them until I get home and can read them with a cup of tea"; "they help me start my week") that continues to grow and looks forward each week to her dose of *thought-provoking, inspirational and entertaining essays to keep you connected with yourself and make sense of this journey called Life.*

To book Kristina for a speaking engagement at your organization or company, or to schedule a private consultation, please contact her through KristinaLeonardi.com .

Made in the USA
Middletown, DE
30 March 2015